Kenelm Henry Digby

Ouranogaia

Heaven and Earth

Kenelm Henry Digby

Ouranogaia
Heaven and Earth

ISBN/EAN: 9783744660068

Printed in Europe, USA, Canada, Australia, Japan

Cover: Foto ©Thomas Meinert / pixelio.de

More available books at **www.hansebooks.com**

OURANOGAIA:

Heaven on Earth.

BY

KENELM HENRY DIGBY.

ὡς αἱ ἡμέραι τοῦ οὐρανοῦ ἐπὶ τῆς γῆς.—Deut. xi. 21.

VOL. I.

London:

[LON]GMANS, GREEN, READER, AND DYER,
PATERNOSTER ROW.
1872.

PREFACE.

The design of this Poem (if such it may be called) is to represent the happiness, comparable in some degree, we might think, to what reigns in Heaven—which results from taking a cheerful, sympathetic, tolerant, and Catholic view of human life, as being on the confines of our celestial country, with constant means of access to it, amidst our various ordinary, or comic, or tragic conditions, hearing and observing with delicate exactitude the most minute things, whether jubilant, or, in a material sense sorrowful, while escaping from impediments to this intense intellectual enjoyment, by mentally merging, as it were, in a confused way, one's own individuality in some other person, or, at least, losing for the time self-consciousness, as if it were others who felt, heard, witnessed, and realized the approach to Paradise. The object is also to suggest that human pleasures in this world, even those which are deemed most strictly confined to earth, and to our twofold formation in the present state of existence, are enhanced immeasurably when associated in a general way with such higher thoughts as may be said, without extravagance, to culminate in Heaven, being tempered and coloured as it were by an all-pervading tone of trust in that forgiveness which constitutes an Article of the Christian Creed.

The whole is so arranged as to show in detail that some of the bliss of Heaven, as far as we can conceive it, may be enjoyed by mankind in this life by means of the spectacle of Creation, and in particular of Beauty, as also Mirth, Admiration, Friendship, Love, Goodness, Peace, Poetry, Learning, Philosophy, the Festivals of the Church, as developing, even by the rites attending them, those internal dispositions which render man what a theologian calls "animal carissimum Deo," and in fine, through sanctity, untroubled and unaffected by human follies, while ignoring, rather than trying to extirpate the inevitable. There is an attempt to show likewise with what effect Heaven may be said to descend especially on youth and age, and on those who have gone astray without having had, as a famous author says, "the foretaste of evil, which is calculation, or its aftertaste alone, which is zero." Poverty, and a low social rank with its consequences, are shown to present no obstacle to this vision of two worlds; and, lastly, Heaven is represented as brought down to the sick and to the dying.

Partly reconstructed, and considerably enlarged, it is presented in this, its definitive form, rather as a new work, which the Author hopes may meet with the same indulgence from a few readers, as he is willing to believe has been shown to his former publications.

CONTENTS TO VOL. I.

	PAGE
Canto I., Heaven brought down on Earth, by the spectacle of Creation	1
Canto II., by Beauty in certain forms	36
Canto III., by other forms	50
Canto IV., by Mirth	58
Canto V., by Admiration (natural objects)	100
Canto VI., by Admiration (works of art, painting, and music)	118
Canto VII., to Youth	155
Canto VIII., to Age	165

Canto IX., by Friendship	174
Canto X., by Love	192
Canto XI., by Goodness	213
Canto XII., to those who have been led astray	257

HEAVEN ON EARTH.

CANTO I.

HEAVEN BROUGHT DOWN ON EARTH BY THE SPECTACLE OF CREATION.

Oh, joy, wing'd guest, how wonderful thou art!
Yes, just as wondrous as the human heart,
Or all that in the universe we see
Replete with wonder and divinity!
Joy at its highest is the lightning's gleam,
Dazzles the sense and passes as a dream.
But then its precious memory can last,
Denoting through what golden gate we pass'd.
And, oh! that moment's glimpse of what's beyond
Once caught—no, never more should we despond.
Besides, as waves still rise and foaming fall,
And one bright breaker seen is never all,

Wave follows wave; the first with sparkling crest
Bursts on the shore, and then in turn the rest,
Again, and still again the lustrous spray,
Lighting the solemn deep and purple way,
The colours of the showery arch brought down,
As if the white-robed pageantry to crown—
So through our life on earth the sadness yields
To raptures rolling from Elysian fields,
Succeeding one another ever fast,
Until, through joy led, we are there at last.
Yes, "there," whatever they or Heav'n may be,
Whose purpose must be true felicity;
For since without a purpose nought we find
The end must there be happiness for mind.
By "there" we mean what all our race has known,
Though Sophists now would its whole sense dis-
    own.—
What Nature dictates by an instinct sure,
What Reason needs must deem a credence pure,
What Christ did promise, nail'd upon the cross,
What gain'd by you, the earth will be no loss.
If more you'd know suffice it must to say
No evil there can for an instant sway.
For creatures rational 'tis no more ill,
'Tis Heav'n, Elysium, name it what you will,
Or Paradise, past Time, a blissful seat,
To satisfy all wants of Beings meet.

The Muse will not exaggerations sing;
Nor are they needed for her potent wing.

Though from its source we trace this tiny rill,
High Heav'n in truth is no less High Heav'n still,
Whose crystal summits no ascent can fear,
However kindred spirits pass them near.
This stream of joy may wind throughout the earth,
Yet not the less in Heav'n it has its birth.
Where All that is, that has been, and will be,
Pours through the universe felicity;
Whose veil by mortals never has been raised,
Whose gifts are felt, who only should be praised!

The earth we deem a vestibule, at best,
Of the bright palace where our souls find rest,
Whose bliss, ne'er flash'd across a poet's dreams,
Effaces Helicon, Hyperion's beams.
The name of man denoted in the Greek
That he a bright higher world than earth should
    seek
A noble language, sprung from noble thought,
But nobler still the truth that here is brought.
For those on whom will shine the World's true
    light
Find that this better world is now in sight,
Within, beside, around them, like the air—
The paradise celestial every where.
So nowhere while we tread this earthly ground
Those terminations can be ever found,
"Where Nature and the world both end," as
    thought
Agricola when British shores he sought.

But onwards farther always than the scene
Which may to sense presented, intervene,
While still accessible and near to mind
A boundless and eternal world we find,
Where we too instantaneously possess
The joys which mortal tongues cannot express;
With which horizon constantly in view
The world we live in wears an aspect new;
As when vast clouds will bound a landscape fair
With forms fictitious, as though Alps were there;
Each grove, each garden, and each structure bright
Becoming thereby glorified to sight!

By many earth is call'd a vale of tears;
And such, in one sense, it for all appears.
By others, who most feel the sorrow deep,
For which the good and evil both must weep,
'Tis found still fraught with things so bright and gay,
That through its paths they would for ever stray.
Some mark but crimes, diseases, follies, woe;
The good that's seen makes other hearts o'erflow
With rapture, admiration, such as speech,
Or song, or painting, nothing e'er can reach.
Then others think the whole perplex'd and strange,
When through its varied walks in mind they range.
What others chiefly love, some cannot bear,
Deem it the poor world's fault that it is fair;
Would have it not restored, and understood
As being never in its fruitage good.—

Never to Heav'n's gate near, another Heav'n,
Whate'er experience may of proofs have given.
Then others analyze its joys, and find
It yields no pleasures for a solid mind.
And yet—and yet there is a voice that cries,
Its acres reach beyond this globe, and rise
To a bright region, where the whole will be
Lost in effulgence of felicity.
These passages abound on every side;
E'en now these golden gates stand open wide,
Whence issue on our life such blissful beams
That e'en within already each one seems,
If only inward life should put forth clear
Visual beams that show to what he's near,
Or songs within us should the while agree
With songs without us from the whole we see,
Dispersing notions mythical of things,
Which to explain them scepticism brings.
Sophists see nought in what surrounds them real!
The most prosaic deem them but ideal.
This form sheer madness sometimes will assume,
And to deny the visible presume,
Receiving ancient friends as in a dream,
E'en telling them they are not whom they seem.
So men who from insanity are far
Will place 'gainst all reality a bar.
" Fanciful! imaginary!" they
To their own secret mind will always say.
True, all that we perceive is still symbolic
In one sense, in accordance e'en with Logic.

We see but the material side of things,
We see not what each noble artist brings—
The spiritual; but whate'er the eye
Beholds, will still excite mysteriously
The clear idea of what is not seen,
However matter's symbols intervene;
While what is not seen gives to all we see
For this clear sense a true reality.
Nathless the Visible, because with veils
Men oft deny where ignorance prevails;
Though that we are, is not from doubt more free
Than that without us are the things we see.
Phantasmal is what they think real most,
And real what they deem an empty boast.
So if you pierce into the depth of things,
The whole is real that your Poet sings.
The Muse will here have nothing more to do
With aught but facts, and with the strictly true.
No Fairy Key she needs here to employ,
To open gates that lead to purest joy.
O strange Realities! nought else will here,
In their most common shapes, surround us near.
Let not the title offer'd lead you wrong,
To deem but Fancy's flight this truthful song,
This simple exposition of a fact,
Though bright, like nature, not the less exact—
Which realizes the Horatian thought
That the whole theme of every Poem ought
To be but " one and simple " in its way;
And that we keep this rule at least you'll say.

Times, it is true, there were when real things
Were only shadow'd in symbolic springs.
But these were then exceptional for man,
When his mysterious course revived, began.
Then, Muse, sing not of types now fled and pass'd,
Nor yet of that which will for ever last—
Reality unveil'd, which Heaven will be
Hereafter in its full felicity.
Reality when veil'd, O Muses, sing,
And to that present joy your incense bring,
That so, no longer we may feel surprise
When things of earth fade into things of skies,
As oft is witness'd, not alone in saints,
But in frail mortals whom no legend paints,
Of whom we too might cry, and not in vain,
" O Races fortunate, Saturnian reign!"

O'er three divisions mankind's life is spread—
The first of types, as of the Jews, is read;
Though even then a Presence could be traced
Which bounds between High Heav'n and earth effaced,
The bliss of future ages to attest,
When all the nations should alike be blest.
But shades, their end accomplish'd, shrank away,
Their night succeeded by our dawning day,
Or what is now Reality while veil'd,
Which dawn commenced when Christian faith prevail'd.

But shadows had the first, as Paul has taught;
To our new age Reality was brought,
Veil'd it is true, but still in substance real,
And not, as some protest, in the ideal
One reign o'er earth's wide bounds and Heav'n above,
All Paradise, subordinate to Love.
Such is the life of mankind upon earth,
When once transferr'd by the mysterious birth;
Having a temple, where each day is seen,
By Faith, in a Form veil'd, th' Eternal Sheen—
That apex of the solemn, mystic vault
Which shines with all the human heart e'er sought.
Reality, thus veil'd, denotes the age
In which men live and act, the earth their stage—
The subject now of my ambitious song,
Including all things that to joy belong.
The third division waits another lyre,
Than all our human thoughts, beyond thought higher;
For there, unveil'd, Reality is seen,
And which from all Eternity has been.
In this sense, therefore, take what I propose,
Whate'er the theme itself demonstrates, shows,
As if to present sight, so bright and clear,
That future life for moments may appear.

These veil'd Realities would make earth Heav'n,
If, with their faith, mankind the whole would leav'n;

For it is but religion they express,
The Christian simply, neither more nor less;
These words, observe, are clear, and common
    plain;
Like Chrysale, therefore, you cannot complain,
That when they're spoken you have then to try
Their meaning to find out and to descry.
If leaven'd not throughout be yet the whole,
That mystery should not confine the soul.
Oh! look, then, for yourself; yes, mark, and see!
Faith would extirpate all this misery—
Each foul, bad thing, that now disturbeth rest,
And bars the gate to you of regions blest,
Of peace, of sweetness, and of purest love,
Which constitute the perfect bliss above.
"But why," you ask, "hath it not leaven'd
    all?"
Say, do you this a grave objection call?
Ask why all seedlings do not rise and grow
To the perfection they were meant to show;
Why the foul worm will taint the beauteous rose,
Why the clear spring not always rises, flows,
Why the wide deep will oft receive the rain,
While hard and dry is left the thirsty plain;
Though no sound mind will question the intent
With which refreshment to the ground is sent.
Yes, you, who would discard all mystery,
Just ask the reason of the things you see:
Why there is sometimes mischief in the air,
To poison life, and blight each thing that's fair;

Why the good tree, that always should yield fruit,
At times bears nought that can its nature suit;
Why birds carnivorous will pounce and prey
Upon the helpless lamb that roves to play—
Ah, my sharp friend, whate'er you deeply know,
This is what you can never, never show.
This opens all the deep, unfathom'd well,
Whose bottom none on earth can ever tell.
So be content with what is daily found,
When that is sweet and to our reason sound;
And let us onwards, singing, to display
From earth to sweet Heav'n the bright, rapid way—
That wide and ample road whose dust is gold,
And pavement stars, as poets e'en behold.
Destructive agencies on earth will stay,
But, with the Theban eagle, soar away
And reach that clime where all is understood
As beautiful and wise, as fair and good.
One object of this flight is to see shine
The lowest things of earth with the divine,
Not to attempt insanely to defile
The latter visions with the coarse and vile;
But rather what's call'd " coarse and vile," to prove
Consistent with what's pure in Heav'n above;
That so the noble soul may not be vex'd,
Or by her poor companion be perplex'd,

But still pass forward on her lofty way,
Through what disparage justly no one may.
Some joys of man can suit but earth below;
Yet Heav'n contrived them; so from thence they
    flow.
You see at once, from viewing thus the whole,
What vistas open to the human soul.
Such are some heights to which our Muse would fly,
Who nature in no parts would vilify—
An honest purpose, though the stern will blame,
The formal hate, and idiots cry out shame.

Great Cicero laments that Homer placed
In Heav'n above what he in man had traced,
And adds, for his part, he would rather crown
The Poet who to man had Heav'n brought down.
That Heav'n begins on earth, our song shall teach,
To show to what great bliss this earth can reach;
That human life, while counting years and time,
May spread the fragrance of another clime.
Ye Muses, fly beyond the mount, and spring,
No more confined to earth with feeble wing,
But pierce the clouds, the blue expanse of air,
And sing the joys we thought were only there.
Show how these oft will secretly descend
And yield to each thing a celestial end;
How common, slight, imperfect earthly things
Can give the human spirit wondrous wings!
How it can find in what is lowest here
A bliss it thought on earth could not be near,

Yes show how in all walks of life around
E'en Heav'n on earth can be already found,
That earth, as another heav'n, is not far,
And even now the gates of heav'n unbar.
Fear not the fate of Tantalus, who dared
Steal from the table where with gods he fared
Their Nectar and Ambrosia for men,
His punishment awarded being then
For that sole crime, as Pindar lets us know;
Since bounteous Heav'n aye loveth to bestow
On mortals here to recompense their love,
The same delights that charm the courts above.
To no Cumæan Sibyl must we speed;
Of no strange conjurations have we need—
Such as famed Paracelsus long did try
And Villeneuve's Arnold, of his secrets shy;
Though Reuchlin and Agrippa will propound
The wonders that with them they thought were found;
Or those of Eastern Magi, from whom came
Mounge, Urgande, fairies, and Morganda's fame.
Of no Hermetic science have we need,
Or cabalistic which could folly breed
Oneiromancy, oldest kind of all,
Which Aristotle vain would never call;
Or Æromancy, which deludes the weak,
We on this truthful path would never seek;
And though we may be said to hold a key,
No divination such we offer thee;

Nor magic squares in which sage Reinard found
Some true instruction, curious and yet sound.
Although as seers we might ourselves proclaim
In sense as true as once was false the name,
An order of phenomena we show
Which leads to " extasy " we surely know.
The universal Panacea we,
Without committing crimes, will offer thee.
Immortal water and divine perfume,
Eternal youth; and, while we nought assume
But what is true, without imagination,
Shall here be yielded by this transmutation,
Which turns to gold and music of the spheres
Whate'er we see, whatever mankind hears;
While not as to the hermit of Kardou
Will joy be shown to be temptation new;
For here Perfection will be found to shine
With pleasure real, and with joy divine.
Then fearlessly abandon to the wind
The fears or doubts that linger in your mind.
With no dark secret, or " illumined " class
Would we to bright Heav'n from the earth now pass.
All men and women, poor and rich the same,
The youth, the child, the aged, we fondly name
Companions of our own on this great quest,
Where all can find true joy, true peace, true rest.
The paths still barr'd to Heav'n will be seen
Far, far below us, dull and dreary, mean,
While, what perhaps is strangest, only found
By those chain'd but by custom to the ground.

Ascent is easy to that upper air,
Let only hearts desire it, and dare.
For day and night the gates stand open wide,
Through which of mortals bless'd can pass the tide;
Each wave to swell the Empire vast of souls,
And glorify the arm that all controls.
For know, whate'er the Stagyrite may say,
Quite instantaneously the soul can stray
Beyond all limits, since, as Bacon said,
A spiritual substance can be sped
As though an Angel through the boundless space,
Since in strict point of fact it needs no place.
All distance corporal is to the soul
Nought; so the mind has entrance to the whole;
And thus escaping from the body's bounds
It reaches here the bless'd Elysian grounds [1].
Here are bright waters, not the Stygian pool;
Here, to assist the sinking is the rule,
That they, at last, may rest in placid seats,
Where each fair angel each new comer greets;
So here, to each one wretched a right hand
Is stretch'd to lift them to the happy strand,
Where they who weeping pass'd their gloomy hours
Are welcomed safe within the glorious bowers;
No gates that open with horrific noise
Are here, but purple wings still fanning joys.
The sounds of Heav'n here float o'er blissful ground,
Where meads of real asphodel are found,

[1] Opus Tertius, cap. 47, 48—50.

The places full of gladness, meadows sweet,
Groves fortunate, and the thrice blessëd seat,
One space of vaster æther, with its light,
And all the happy spirits given to sight;
To none a home exclusive, all in one,
For ever flying through the glory won;
Through the wide fields of life-eternal's air,
Gazing for ever on the good and fair.
Such, from these gates of horn, is now the way;
While some, for nought, most wantonly will stray
Through the false shining ivory doors of doom,
To find a darkness other than the tomb.

Fear not, O heart! as if you here can meet
Sophistic dreams or palpable deceit.
Nought that surpasses human measure here—
Urania sings but what to all is clear.
'Tis plain and common sense that I invoke
What no fair maidens ever will provoke;
A fact important to remark for me,
Whose theme seems false without their company.
And would be false; since if they had not been
In Eden's garden good had not been seen;
And rather would I that my book lay shut
Within a woman's casket (only cut)
Than open in a scholar's study, where
Like Euphues, to see it I've no care.
Pretence, or things unproved you will not meet,
Or speculative themes however sweet.

And no dark, sly magician will you find,
Who with false visions would mislead your mind,
Like him we read of, with his garden fair,
Who victims made of those who enter'd there.
Within that high enclosure there were found
What seem'd fair fruits and flowers growing round;
But, strange to add, he there would none admit,
Excepting foes, or some devoid of wit;
For whom, with words alluring, then he threw
The gates wide open, to entice their view.
Once enter'd there, the wonder was to see
How each did prize it as felicity;
Though from the first they all were brought to know
The whole to be a vain and empty show.
Still there, though restless, would they aye remain,
And, while they chose to stay, would yet complain,
And even yield their whole inheritance
To him who did their spirits so entrance;
They deem'd it Paradise that still would yield
The fruits immortal of th' Elysian field.
Like poor pain'd alchemists in days of yore,
Most wretched, who on crucibles would pore,
Disdaining to look farther, or beyond
The false enclosure and its poison'd bond;
Until the dark magician, who did scoff
His victims so enchanted, cut them off;

And the factitious Eden proved to be
A glade of pains, and death, and misery!
But such grave fables even can deceive.
Experience judges better far than Eve,
And teaches to detect all hollow seeming,
And recognize it as deceptive dreaming—
So false was old Quarles when he sung to tell,
" A seeming Heaven is the way to Hell."
The seeming way to pleasure is the right;
For no false semblance long misleads the sight,
Though " double-gilded as the doors of day,"
The proud, fantastic gates invite to stray.
No, trustless heart, what seems here is the truth,
The sovereign good of man in age or youth.
Not that once widely-famed Atlantic Isle,
Which the wise man of Saïs did beguile,
Till, hearing him, sage Solon would relate
In verse the bliss of that ideal state;
Though leaving his description incomplete,
To furnish still a similar defeat
When Plato even, who would seize the theme,
Unfinish'd left it as a passing dream;
Nought else for us imperfect to be found
In all his writings but that fancied ground.
Nor are we vainly trying to portray
The joys imagined of an ancient day,
To sing " the Islands Fortunate " of those
Who there the fields Elysian did suppose,
Seats of the bless'd, which the barbarians thought
Might off the shore of Africa be sought,

c

Which Homer sung, Sertorius wish'd to see,
From wars and men despotic ever free,
Where he with perfect peace might ever dwell,
And find the whole around him right and well—
Mere fruitless efforts of men's anxious mind,
What we would sing of, realized to find.
To show that Heav'n on earth can now descend,
Is not, like them, to seek a hopeless end.
It is but truth to point out and maintain,
And simply tell how bliss on earth can reign.
The real Paradise is here in view,
As old as Innocence, yet ever new,
Whose wholesome fragrance doth perfume the ground
Where real fruits and flowers bloom around.

Oh, Science, 'tis not thee I have to fear,
If now my song should meet thy cautious ear!
It is thine enemy, thy bane as well,
Who scoffs and contradicts what now I tell;
'Tis Inattention, that most fatal foe
To all the bliss on earth, I now would show.
But let her hence, and seek her senseless way,
While thou, O Science, will to hear me stay;
For though thou mayst not often wander so,
Content, if things material thou shouldst know,
As through the heights or depths of Nature's bounds
Thou passest and dost heed not other sounds,
No wonders real yield offence to thee,
And thou wilt own the first that mystery

Agrees with what thou never canst deny,
Howe'er enskied they are, above all high.
Experience thou wilt always count a fact,
Though sung by Muses, not the less exact.
Analysis may chiefly suit thy head;
But this bright theme need not that method dread;
Though when applied to life as seen around
Life's purpose ceases while its depths are found;
So here you may all vital movement kill,
But truth immortal it remaineth still.

But will the simple hearts that most I love
Be moved so high an object to approve?
I know that themes beyond a hearer's sphere
At first will seldom please, and strange appear;
And hence they all must now proportion'd be
To the small minds that serve publicity;
But still the Muse will hope e'en these will find
Her theme at last congenial with their mind;
For by degrees at least they will perceive
What want of thought had made them doubt or leave;
Since Sentiment most found in simple hearts
When so directed views like these imparts.
For here, I nought invent; I but dispose,
And give a new form to what each one knows,
As Architects find marble on the hill:
With which they then construct whate'er they will.

But now to me, no Sibyl, thou wilt say,
Like the Virgilian hero, " Teach the way,
Show us the sacred doors," that we may fly,
And all the wonders they unfold descry.
But much we doubt that thou a path canst find
On earth to reach the Paradise for mind.
Since men the highest placed, who watch the most,
Appear to deem this but an empty boast.
They send us back to Perrault's tales again,
And seem to say those hopes are wholly vain.
Upon their high tower fix'd, like Sister Anne,
To teach despair is simply all they can.
The world spread round them wears no aspect new;
No real Paradise appears in view.
Alas! by them there's nothing ever seen
" But sun and dust, or grass still growing green."
Well, take your answer; and no more deny
That Heav'n on earth to us is ever nigh.

Then first our eyes can see, our hands can feel
What does the mind and work of God reveal,
Who hath dispensed His bounties here on earth
As in the heavens, causing angels' mirth;
Diffusing fragrance through the vernal air,
While flowers will whisper in each garden fair,
From whence they stole their perfume and array,
Which can their Maker by His art display;
For present still in valley and in plain,
He in this Eden new is seen again,

Who thus creates the trefoil, cinqfoil too,
As if He counted while He wrought, like you;
For so the smallest, tritest thing we see
Proclaims the Fiat of Divinity—
As loudly as the planets that we trace,
Or unnamed suns, in boundless, unknown space.
To any mortal of attentive mind,
Who is not intellectually blind,
The fact, not only visible, is such,
That palpable, 'tis subject to our touch,
Attesting, in accordance with the voice
Of cherubim, all creatures to rejoice,
That Heav'n not only, but the earth as well
" Proclaims the glory " which the angels tell.
But at the sound of such a herald's cry
The earth makes part of that bright region high.

A sense of Nature's beauty when profound
Denotes a mind most intimately sound.
O sage antiquity! what tales thou hast,
While seldom equall'd, ne'er by us surpass'd!
What can exceed the glory of that trait,
When in reply the sage had nought to say
To Alexander, charging him to ask
Some gift, but that the king should spare the task,
Requesting that he would but step aside,
From him no longer there the sun to hide,
Nor intercept the landscape where he sat;
He had nought else to ask from him but that!

Trite and familiar anecdote, but grand,
When we its whole deep meaning understand;
For Nature of herself can even see
At least the borders of felicity;
Although the streams that from those limits glide
Alpheus like at times their flow will hide,
Again to issue forth and reappear,
As when their bright crystalline source was near.
And hence the joys of leisure, for a mind
That will, attentive, such a rapture find,
As even with the ancients, we are told,
In most laborious men we oft behold,
Can yield a passage ever, more or less,
To joys which we in words cannot express.
Whate'er the total lot of men may be,
Its isolated gifts with joy agree;
And so, apart from memory and fear
The present will man's moment best appear.
Such words each keen observer will employ
To notice thus our instantaneous joy.
Moments dissever'd wholly from the past
And future which are ne'er with aught o'ercast,
As painted on the wise poetic page
Of Tick describing his young artist's age,
Replete with transports known in every station,
Which draw from keen De Staël the exclamation,
" What wonders thus surround us every where,
Of which e'en we ourselves are not aware!"
The future breaks in joy no heart divines;
But each detach'd, successive moment shines,

Which simple hearts are open to receive,
While Pride alone suspects they may deceive.
Although, as Horace says, Arcadians we
Have nought to do with what regards the sea,
Like Scipio and Lælius on the shore,
We draw near Paradise still more and more;
Like Scævola, our leisure being wise,
We play on earth, conversant with the skies;
" Ease is the sauce of labour," said a sage.
With that at times life's tedium we assuage.
Like Socrates, obnoxious to the jest
Of Alcibiades disdaining rest,
We still can find in leisure what we feel
Must a supernal joy to man reveal;
For these sweet pleasures more or less must flow
From works divine; and that is all we know.

But with God's works surrounded, to live here
Is thus far Heav'n; and, besides, 'tis clear,
What men already know who search their mind
Surpasses all that on this earth we find.
Yes, traverse slowly now that spacious hall,
And its vast wealth divine will you appal.
For who bestow'd that? whence is it derived?
Your Maker; and to Him it be ascribed.
A thirst for knowledge without seeing this
Is a true end of knowledge but to miss;
To thirst for it as e'en would Diderot,
And only ever thirstier to grow.

But this is simply not to be a man,
Contracting thus his own allotted span.

In the heart, conscience, words announced for ears,
Before our face great Nature's Book appears;
And in that last immense and beauteous page
We see, we feel, and hear what can assuage
The instinct which impels us to desire
Something than all this earth, much purer, higher,
The view of things created, which unites
The ground we tread on with celestial sights.
As in the vales of Heav'n, we here can greet,
Our country's confines and our ancient seat.
This is affirm'd by Bernard—many more,
Anthony, of Padua, famed of yore,
Spain's Villanova's Thomas, and of schools,
The angel, who for aiding sight gives rules,
Prescribing how, and by what means we see
In Nature's face high Heav'n's great mystery.
That Nature's Author does by vision speak
Is proved, if in ourselves alone we seek.
Vision is His Language unto man,
Let him explain the mystery who can.
" When learn'd we its alphabet?" demands
The sage who its diffusion understands.
We only know, intuitive perceptions
Which never lead the weakest to deceptions,

Arise from adaptations made, past doubt,
Of things within us to things found without,
From pre-establish'd harmony that reigns
Between the soul and Nature's wide domains,
By means of which, from feelings, we can read
The language which reveals what we all need—
A knowledge of the laws and operations
Of the external world, through all mutations.
"Oh, what a wond'rous book!" the Spaniard cries,
"What deep Theology within it lies!
What beauty in each page we always trace
Of things here visible to all our race!"
And then what echoes through the lofty whole,
As if from voices, to direct the soul
Heav'nward still! though even in this earth's bower
Are seen the works of the Creator's power.
Theocritus could sing this beauty well;
Though whither led it, he did never tell.
Dark rocks, blue mountains with the icy peak,
The tragic Muse of old was found to seek.
To forests, flowery meads would oft repair
The Idyl-loving Bard, and Heaven was there;
Although of genius he might feel the sting,
His cure by that reveal'd he did not sing.
Yet there was it extended, bright and calm,
The joy of innocence, of grief the balm.
Then, too, in Nature's face we here may find
An image of the heaven for our mind.
For, oh! that silence of the verdant wood,
What vistas there, if rightly understood;

That "morning humour 'neath Verona's grove"
Denotes the heart that farther still should rove.
Then life itself, so great a mystery,
Of which the action we both feel and see—
Life, which no science ever can explain,
Can lead on our minds to Heav'n thus again.
In biologic studies some may rest,
To Heav'n fly others whose content is best.

But Beauty, above all, discloses most
What fires with joy the great artistic Host
Of those who, if they cannot paint as well,
Reflect in mind the thoughts no tongue can tell.
Oh Beauty, high Heav'n's secret, ray divine!
Whence comest thou? What mortal can opine?
Why must we love thee, oh what man can tell
Why are we drawn to thee as by a spell,
As magnets draw the iron? Why must we
To thy attraction thus so docile be?
Embrace thy shadow, to thy kisses fly,
Or from thee torn must weep and fade and die?
None know thy secret; all thy empire own;
At thy bright aspect more than earth is shown.
We only know that thy great fascination
Must of our instincts be the revelation [1].

Consider only beauty of the earth,
Which e'en to thoughts divine can here give birth.

[1] Lamartine.

What is that vale of Tempe but a way
Through which e'en disembodied souls would
    stray?
Or view the source of Ladon, with its stream,
Bright Aroanius, an Arcadian dream.
See those clear floods of azure near the shore,
Where faithless men, you'd say, would e'en adore,
Such as that lake from which imperial eyes
Could never turn—great symbol for the wise—
And then that golden dawn, that ruddy west,
Reveal the portals through which man finds rest,
Which Homer's heroes seem to have descried
While " gazing on, or into Heaven wide."

    When Summer has come so bright
        All Nature with joy is clad;
    The smile of God seems to light
        On creatures to make them glad.
    Each field, each grove has its part;
        The sky over all pours bliss;
    The wood gives ears to your heart,
        The wave to the shore its kiss.
    'Tis the invisible glows,
        Under its vault of bright sapphires,
    A stream from Eden that flows
        To the soft music of zephyrs.
    The Summer's bright morn is fire,
        The day to effulgence given,
    Eve will in glory expire,
        Night is a vision of Heav'n.

> Yes, God is at all times here;
> Saith Hugo, in Lyric strain,
> For Spring, Autumn, Winter drear
> Have pageants to hail his reign.

Then dense is he who cannot understand,
How all things solemn, beautiful, and grand
Disclose a view of that celestial Power
Which rules all beings past the mortal hour;
And, sooth, not "happy now" "the man," we cry,
"To whom great Pan and Silvánus are nigh,"
Or who can say, "How oft the Nymphs of groves
And lakes have cheer'd the lonely wight who roves"?
But happy he who sees beyond all plains
The blissful hills where no one more complains!
Who sees, as Samson wish'd, through every pore,
The scenes consummate prompting to adore,
His sight, like feeling, through all parts diffused,
As if to Heav'n's enchantment he were used.
In fine, this earth extendeth even there,
By means of histories of things that were,
As of those sages, separate to God,
Whose blessëd feet its plains and paths have trod.
Ideas, when associated so,
Them will before us bring and clearly show.
On mountains and in woods Mind sees the cell
Of men who thus on earth in Heav'n did dwell.
The tree, the flower, the rock stand not alone;
Their friends it sees when meditative grown,

By thinking on that beauty even there
Which led these sages to a higher air.
For all this joy and beauty in the face
Of Nature, which we thus can daily trace,
Were felt by saints, great Basil, and the rest,
Who, with Augustine, farther sought the best.
Though in the Pagan writers we ne'er find
A trace of what this yieldeth to our mind.
Pausanias will describe each grove and hill;
Cold and unmoved he vieweth beauty still.
His dry details suggest what must be there;
We long to visit sites so grand and fair.
Oh, with what rapture would I always fly
To see what there he says can meet the eye!
This rock projecting, and that winding glade,
The road which mounts where olives cast their shade;
But all this beauty picturesque remains
For him unknown and unexplored domains.
One instance only of this sense is found
Where Scylax the known world would visit round.
He says, " Pellene, rising from the sea,
In Macedonia towers with majesty."
The Christians first appear to have survey'd
Hills, groves, and lakes as all with beauty made;
As though a sense before unfelt by men
The Picturesque had first awaken'd then.
Where former men had pass'd observing nought,
These see the hand that raised high Heav'n's vault;
Who will'd that rays from distant orbs should yield
The beauteous colours of the earthly field.

Creation then disclosed on every side,
The courts celestial open near and wide,
Comprising earth and all that's known below,
To what side e'er we turn, where'er we go.
For why are useless flowers all clad so fair
While things most useful earthly raiment wear?
'Tis that the beautiful may point to Heav'n,
For which end chiefly is it ever given.
The use of plants nutritious each one knows,
This is the use of Lilies and the Rose.
With minds directed thus to Nature's face
The happy garden reaches to each place.

While living, still with present mortal sight,
Having left neither men nor this sweet light,
'Tis Heaven we see; and one short moment's glance,
Beyond all speech, can human minds entrance.

But let us now distinguish, choose some parts,
To mark how Heav'n can thus be in our hearts;
Which sphere must yield at least analogy
With all the good that on this earth we see.
What, if things God on earth in Heav'n has wrought
Be like each other more than oft is thought?
'Tis proved, they say, that all the Planets show
The same materials as this globe below,
Which indicates a likeness in them all,
By whatsoever names these worlds we call.

If the same gas and minerals are there,
There may be likewise what on earth is fair,
Intensified perhaps, but, in the main,
What can a certain sameness still sustain
With gladness and with beauty, such as here
To flow from God and Heaven must appear.
But even if the distant worlds we see
With perfect beauty should not all agree,
The nearer we approach to the unseen
The more intense, we know, must be the sheen.
For beauty here derives its charms alone
From what it represents, as sages own.
So Heav'n, where God unseen does ever dwell
Must be of beauty pure th' eternal well.
The property of beauty is to cause
Pleasure and joy by force of unknown laws.
Judgment with pleasure ever will unite
To swell the blissful tide that flows so bright.
Its source is not the sentiments that rise
To dictate ever where self-interest lies.
The Beautiful and Useful e'en must be
Each sole in mind and rule with sovereignty.
Strange mystery of Nature! quite alone
Will Beauty reign, and claim hearts for her own.
And whither are we led when docile so?
To Paradise, from which this joy must flow.
For know, as all things visible reveal
The things unseen which Nature would conceal,
So all the beautiful that we behold
Flows from the beautiful unseen, untold.

The sheen, invisible to human eyes,
Is the sole fountain that to us supplies
The beautiful in Nature as in Art;
And unseen beauty thus can move our heart
Esthetically e'en. Cut off that spring,
Nor Art nor Nature can produce a thing
That moves us with a sense of beauty so
Without regard to interest here below.
And hence it is, that as we onward stray
Some thoughtful sages would oppose the way,
Crying, with Jouffroy, that this passion keen
For Beauty here has dangers quite unseen;
Yea, none more dangerous he will maintain
Than such a passion which is spent in vain;
Since this great want of beauty for the eye
Can't here be satisfied, howe'er we try.
While soul and body are so close allied
This highest satisfaction is denied.
It is the pledge, he thinks, of future life,
And so may cheer us 'midst the mortal strife.
But if it should absorb us in desire,
It yields emotions that perplex and tire.
The Beautiful as such is all divine,
And wholly upon earth it will not shine;
But then, what's call'd sublime with struggles bound
As human ever on the earth is found.
The fundamental source of the sublime
Is the great struggle that belongs to time.
The pleasure that it yields is not the same
As that which unto us from Beauty came.

This last is all divine, beyond our strife;
The former suits alone our present life.
" Choose then the path," he cries; which joy secures,
Struggle, contend, the true sublime is yours.
Let gleams of beauty still direct your way,
But think not that with you they long can stay.
Though still some steps we take while here below,
To follow rays which thus from Heav'n will flow."
   " This love of beauty," saith a sage,
Whose writings glow at every page,
" Of man is an essential part,
When he enjoys a healthy heart,
Or human nature whole and sound,
In which it ever will be found.
At times, with faults that love has stood,
But in itself 'tis wholly good;
Of Envy, Avarice, and Care
The deadly foe, and sure to dare
Resist all cruelty," which shows
The origin from which it flows,
And whither it would lead us, till
In Eden's fields we found its rill.
Say, what is beauty but a sun
In whose bright ray is Heav'n begun?
Yes, in all the trees and flowers,
Placid lakes and woodbine bowers,
Slopes and lawns, the mountain grove,
Heights to which we still would rove,
Bubbling streams and daisied grass—
All that will in charm surpass,

As in sweet Aosta's vale,
Mantled with the olive pale,
We experience what was meant
By what man did not invent.
Haste but alone to France with me,
Where skies inspire felicity.
No sudden streams of damp raw air,
Like false notes in a concert fair,
Will interrupt the calm delight
With which you gaze on what is bright.
The atmospheric joy will seem
To make whate'er you see a dream.
The sunrise on a summer's morn,
When Nature will herself adorn
As for a fête, while earth will wear
A certain novel aspect there—
The ground a Paradise, each spot
Teeming with what is ne'er forgot;
A something you have read about,
Of which the charm is not found out;
An influence of light and air
Producing what is nameless fair;
As towards the south you gaily stray,
And Heav'n descends upon your way,
And the sweet chime of early bells
The truth of all your feeling tells—
These incidents of warmer climes
Transport you elsewhere thus at times.
But, wherever artists stray,
Beauty smiles upon their way.

See the dawn that comes with speed,
While on moors the stags will feed,
Purple veil that flies the morn,
Crescent moon with slender horn,
Bright Aurora's steeds foreshown
By a faint but golden tone,
Stars of spring that fade away
At cerulean tints of day,
Dews and air perfumed around—
Sweet Heav'n in them all is found;
For such beauty marks the plan
Meant for creatures and for man.
How can it be ever past?
Elsewhere too it needs must last
In some form, or tone right fair,
Though incomparable there.
So when we enjoy its sheen,
Somewhat of Heav'n here is seen.
But Beauty comes in still more radiant vest,
As in the human countenance express'd,
Which some think is the shade or carnal trace
Of the Profiles of the Eternal Face.
In this are many forms, proclaiming each
That Heav'n on earth is now within our reach.
Here, too, we see what God deems good and fair;
Resemblance to it must be likewise there;
So that e'en Science, using prose aright,
Might say angelic forms are here in sight.

"The beautiful and good[1]" can never be
So wholly different from what we see;
Though here, no doubt, 'tis moulded by the tone
Which human minds, in states that differ, own.

  Where the child sits smiling so,
  Where the maiden's graces flow,
  Where the youth will laugh and play,
  Where old age will cheerful stay,
  Airs from Heav'n perfume the way.

  Eden never can be far,
  No gates stand we need unbar,
  When the sight of earthly sheen,
  Acting on sensations keen,
  Makes us love what is unseen.

CANTO II.

BY BEAUTY IN CERTAIN FORMS.

O Muse of Raphael, Francia, be near,
That what my mind has seen may now appear!
While, thoughtful, e'en with thee I onwards stray,
Revolving beauty that has pass'd away—
From sight at least, though ever to remain
Within my soul, to prompt the pensive strain.

  [1] καλὸν κἀγαθόν.

Let's mark three forms, as modified by change
Of circumstances in their mortal range,
Clothed with sweet sadness, as I think and sing,
And stretch for bright Heav'n a confiding wing,
Where all can meet again, together soar,
And where of parting we shall hear no more.

The first denotes the sorrow of this earth,
Though not concealing whence it owes its birth.

Hence, grim unmeaning gloom,
The sickly vapours of a vacant heart,
Which ever will impart
A shade that mind will shroud, and rest on it to loom!
And fill its eyes with grief
Which can be felt, but never quite explain'd:
Such dulness is sustain'd
By those whose soul is chill'd, as by a spell
Whose source they cannot tell,
While wantonly they will reject relief.
  But welcome, O thou pensive maid!
  Like the summer's twilight shade,
  That kindlest thoughts with such a smile
  As can vague sorrow e'en beguile
  With gleams of Heaven, as in the West
  Still lingers brightness, while the rest
  Is shrouded with the pall of night,
  That only sky should meet the sight
  To lure us upwards to the plains
  Where joy unchequer'd aye remains.

Her did I lately straying see,
To dwell thenceforth in memory.

  Why are those sweet smiles sad?
   Those eyes that speak?
  When joys can soon be had
   Which she does seek?
  " Yes, joys, but not to last!"
   And she is weak
    For others.

  Why does her gladness fly
   From day to day,
  As lightning leaves the sky,
   Nor longer stay?
  She oft has lost the track—
   Sweet Eden's way,
    That flowers.

  But let that path be found,
   And then she strays
  Through joys that play around
   Those blissful ways;
  Her wish at last is crown'd
   With heavenly rays—
    Love's bowers.

How strange, familiar names to hear,
When visions like this first appear!

But even such did lately show
To my mind's eye ne'er thence to flow,
When straying to Kilburnia's hill.
Met only once, I see her still;
For in her half-glad, thoughtful look,
I read, as in a mystic book,
How, made for joy, e'en here on earth,
To her might come the angels' mirth.
Her large and pensive eyes did pierce
Through me, as through the universe;
And like an ocean was the roll
Of thought in them from her deep soul;
And yet it sounded, so to say,
Like tolls for an eternal day;
For, sooth, it only sounded love,
Which reigns unchequer'd up above.
True, it still told of sadness here;
Formosa knows what is a tear;
That joys are short and sorrows long,
Is still the burden of her song.
They who are crying when she cries
Must often cry with no surprise.
But to her solemn, quiet thought
Is doubtless all Heav'n often brought.
The Stagirite of her would say
Dramatic interest in her lay,
From being as if nothing wholly,
Not one or other, and that solely,
Still partly willing, partly not,
Still pleased, and grieving at her lot,

Whose cause of sorrow might be sought
In some mistake, or human fault,
Not in a will perverse, as where
There is a soul that crime would dare.
She reach'd her lonely dwelling so;
And more of her I did not know.
It was a dark autumnal eve
When me, for ever, she did leave.
That small house look'd deserted, poor,
But Heav'n might oft be there, I'm sure.
For airs from Heav'n would welcomed be
Within those walls, it seem'd to me,
Who, on her ne'er forgotten face
Could somewhat more than beauty trace.
Tall trees did shade the dwellings near,
Which made its garden sad appear;
A shelter'd, placid, pensive plot;
The Nymphs would there have found their grot;
Since near it is a mineral well
Of which the ancients much could tell.
But for these thoughtful, loving eyes,
E'en a better charm therein lies—
The thoughts of love in idleness,
The wish her words could ne'er express,
A vague and half-developed thought,
Longing for what the best have sought.
A pensive aspect the whole bore,
Like hers who pass'd within the door;
But still there may be calm most holy
In times of tender melancholy,

Divinest, it is even call'd
By poets sage, while unappall'd;
As if 'twere meant to temper thus
The greatest things reserved for us,
Descended from celestial height
In mercy to the human sight,
That thoughts fraught with felicity
Might blind not our humanity,
Too weak without such veils to view
Heav'n's brightness in unclouded hue.
"Well, but then, tell me," said a maid,
"Whom this small portrait pensive made:
Hast thou ne'er seen her there again?"
I think her life is steep'd in pain.
No, never. All seems lonely there,
Deserted, not a footstep rare.
The houses, half-unfinish'd, stand
As if for them were no demand;
I think she must have left the spot,
As not contented with her lot.
"Ah, poor Formosa!" then she cried;
"No, her my heart cannot deride."
And yet, still farther as she strays,
Who knows what beauty she surveys?
Since her lone sadness may find rest,
And lead her yet to what is best.
Wise Crashaw's lines I'd imitate,
To paint her smiling, thoughtful state.
With his sweet song in memory,
A kind of plagiarist I'd be.

All joy would be more joy for us,
If pensive e'en we could mourn thus;
If at each sigh, and prompt to fall,
We felt what she a bead might call.
For in her half-unconscious woe,
Her tears, as well as years, will flow.
From such a poet she would hear
Nought but these words, "Bright Heav'n is near.'
He'd make her pillow with the down
Of angels' wings; and, for her crown,
He'd ask but of her tears a store,
Changed to what sparkles ever more.
Even if she had not stray'd,
Pensive we might both be made;
For such beauty cannot stay
Any where; it steals away,
Homesick, to its natal bower,
Frighten'd at Time's swift-sped hour.
To-day its smiles you may have won;
To-morrow, where? 'tis fled and gone;
'Tis a sunbeam, 'tis a bird
Singing, for a moment heard;
A flow'ret on the field in May,
Closed in a week, or mow'd away;
'Tis a leaf that needs must fly
When the summer too will die;
'Tis at eve a golden cloud,
Which the night so soon will shroud;
'Tis a dew-drop on the rose,
Vanishing at morning's close;

'Tis but a wave that glows to sight
With playful Iris, colour'd bright;
'Tis the deep raptures of a thought,
Of which no word expresses aught;
'Tis joy's swift acme; 'tis whate'er
Smiles in the spring or summer air,
As speeding from you it will cry,
" Oh, follow me, to Eden fly!"

The second bright form, so fair and free,
From Heav'n descends, Euphrosyne.
She comes with mirth, and graces too,
To prove what true heart's-ease can do;
As frolicsome as summer's wind,
Or what spring breathes, will be her mind.
But what is youthful jollity,
Which in her pranks and jests you see,
Unless a sprite from Heav'n here sent
By Him who wills our merriment?
Hence, thou affected mirth that chills
More deeply than all frozen rills!
Hence, laughter like hyæna's note,
That issues from an impious throat!
Hence, wiles that seek to send asleep
Dull care, and make it still more deep!
But come, O form of angels bright,
That charms the ear, enchants the sight,
The maiden, innocent and free,
That breathes true joy and liberty!

HEAVEN ON EARTH.

Yes, dance, and sing, and fling away
The trammels of a darksome sway
That seeks on earth to counteract
The clearest, and divinest fact!
For since Heav'n's sons did shout with joy,
Sing should the maiden and the boy;
And when they sing, and dance around,
A trace of Heav'n on earth is found.
Such knew I, Mary, know I still,
Fulfilling their wise Maker's will,
By casting all around them here
A joy which still brings bright Heav'n near;
On the green hill, or in the wood,
Where vie with them no linnet could;
In the sweet shade or on the stream,
Where mirth surpass'd what you could dream;
In the house, around the fire,
Where the rain we'd e'en admire;
Under fragrant thorns of May,
Out for a whole summer's day;
Or, if they would but stroll with me
In farthest nook of Finsbury,
Where in a verdant angle ends
The Park near which the river wends.
The Summer, Winter, Autumn, Spring,
They fann'd with such a gladsome wing,
That each time present seem'd the best
To yield both hearts and minds their rest.
And what can be such feelings then,
But joys meant elsewhere, too, for men?

Such unreprovëd pleasures free,
In part disclose eternity,
Where joy is endless without measure,
And nought but pure, protracted pleasure,
Begun on earth, complete above,
Where there is no death for love.

But now the third form must inspire our song.
To holy Beauty show what does belong.
What oft great Homer's lofty Muse does grace,
I surely may have leave to name and trace;
Nor would Euripides himself disdain
When lowly damsels occupy my strain.
For all the old tragedians justly loved
To paint to life these servants unreproved,
Whose virtues, such as formerly could be,
They sweetly sing, and show with joy to thee.
The daughter of Alcinous would go
To frolic on the beach attended so;
Her maidens from the Graces had obtain'd
A beauty which their modesty sustain'd.
With them, their work accomplish'd, would she play,
And wile the sweet hours of a summer's day;
Nor e'er without the twain of beauteous hair
Would she her chariot drive to wander there.
Their smooth white arms would the great Poet sing;
As woodland Nymphs, they struck with awe the King,

Who, while upon the shore he wearied lay,
Remark'd how frighten'd they did trip away;
As the white fawns will always farther fly
When aught not quite familiar meets their eye.
Their goodness by obedience was implied,
Attending her, still ever at her side,
Yet with arch words encouraging each other,
While maiden innocence all else would smother.
And must a later Muse disdain to show
What Heaven on damsels such can now bestow?
Who not, as Nymphs, can dazzle human sight,
But awe the hardest, as pure angels bright,
Their duty and obedience still their aim,
Pure simple goodness, without spot or shame.
No, truly, let that scorn now shun my lyre;
It only suits those dames who nought admire.
The Romans e'en might shame us if we thought
That ne'er to mention such our Poets ought.
Their servant-maidens had their laughing fête
Their noble daring to commemorate;
When, fair Tutulæ at their head, they went
On saving Romans from the Latins bent,
Sped to the camp, convey'd away the swords
Of foes who thus became disarmëd hordes.
And what are all such victories when we
More than Camilla's moral courage see
In girls who now, with nature at their side,
Their faith proclaim and all their virtues hide?

Then Beauty, bold and free, by hidden power
Still guarded, humbly trips forth from her bower
In person of an humble maid, who speeds
To join the throng that Vesper office heeds,
To sing Davidic Psalms. She goes alone,
But lackey'd by plumed angels, who will own
That she in her free, servile state is high
In the great roll of Heaven's nobility.
That hidden majesty I lately felt
When at her side with others there I knelt,
Admiring, e'en surprised, and half aghast,
To find, as elsewhere, how I was surpass'd
In feeling e'en; and for nought else can I
E'er hope to win a moment's sympathy.
'Twas in St. James's chapel, near the door,
Where of such holy faces there is store;
Her feast of nectar'd sweets is in the song
That to the hour of Vesper does belong;
The chanting of sweet Psalmody and sound
Of organs had the silence broke around.
List, list! I hear her voice that now will sing
The words in Latin of great Israel's King;
Her book is closed; she knows these songs by heart;
It serves but to denote the anthem's part
Which changes as the office may require;
And she will ever sing still with the choir,
Thus adding to its loud and solemn tone
An enskied thrilling echo of her own.
Now here again was Heaven on earth display'd
Before the eyes of this poor lowly maid,

As she pass'd on with majesty, to scare
All evil things that injure her would dare.
So awful goodness will appear to men,
Thus arm'd with innocence as shining then;
For briskly then she rose, and tripp'd along,
As soon as finish'd was the evening song,
Homewards; and there, whatever home might be,
Did, and must, reign Heav'n's own felicity.
Yes, still through Heav'n must walk this saintly
    maid—
In Heav'n her home, her path, her bed is made;
Whether, with beauty clad, and comely dress,
She trips more gaily than can words express,
Or, formally directed to the sky,
With what she feels the earth can never vie.
On ground she treads, but like a lark to soar—
Inhaling joy, she sings at Heav'n's bright door.
No ancient scaly-headed Gorgon shield
Does this untutor'd saintly maiden wield;
No gloomy frowns of sour severity
Disturb her gay and bright serenity;
But in her tranquil looks still shines the grace
That she has learn'd in that hallow'd place:
The air of Paradise does winnow round
Each path she follows, howsoever found.
In hours of mirth, of work, of silence, prayer,
It is not earth, but it is Heav'n that's there.

Then later, elsewhere, I beheld advance
Some refugees flown, stripp'd of all, from France.

But, oh! remark that damsel, as you pass,
Who, on the day of All Saints, hears the Mass.
What a bright contrast to the world around!
In her what radiance from Elysian ground!
It needs no Poet's fancy there to trace
Heav'n's eight beatitudes on that sweet face.
Not wanting one—as if intoned were all,
Clear as from altars the soft, gracious call.
There on those finely-chisell'd features lie
The sweet mysterious secrets of the sky—
The poverty of spirit, meekness dear,
The grief which seeks to hide its falling tear;
The thirst for justice in a holy breast;
The mercy blessing, while itself is blest:
The innocence of heart on which we know,
God will the vision of Himself bestow;
The peace, and then, to bear all the endeavour,
Ah, seen but once, you can forget it never!
The bird when fascinated cannot fly;
So stood I there; that spell-bound bird was I.
Our common country, seen, my thoughts had raised,
And so, from all else rapt, I stood and gazed.

Great charmer of the mind, sweet Beauty's light,
With thee a world much fairer is in sight
Than this poor earth, if bars should intervene
To hide from view the true, eternal sheen.

CANTO III.

BY OTHER FORMS.

O HEAVENLY Muse, Urania, Love thou art,
Who, singing beauty, canst thus teach our heart!
But what are words or songs? one glance of eyes
Their skill, or sweetest harmony defies.

Beauty in other forms, that all can know—
Nathless, the Muse inspiring, we would show.
Unawed by Milton who its force e'en finds
To be "in th' admiration of weak minds."
There is the dauntless, noble spirit, bold,
Whose acts heroic history oft has told.
There is the humble being, tender, fond,
Knowing well Love, but nothing else beyond;
Knowing that she knows not, quiet, blest,
And finding in that ignorance true rest.
There is the nervous, diffident, and shy,
Who fears to show her love, she knows not why;
Most equitable, just, who cares for others,
Oft shunn'd by some, the life and soul of mothers,
With childlike smiles that deck her Raphael face,
Though steps, through sorrows long, she had to trace.
There is the perfect shape where blemish lies,
Which rather bringeth liking to the eyes,
In every way than loathing to the mind,
In any way as Euthues did find.

CANTO III.

There is the maid whom science does inspire
To watch the stars, and works of God admire;
There is another who delights to sing,
And skim o'er life with brightly-colour'd wing.
There is the smiling arch one, fond of fun,
Whose mirth by slightest incidents is won;
Brave, candid, merry on the public way,
Who to her friend has always much to say;
Who strokes his horse, and e'en admires his spur,
As if it waken'd chivalry in her;
Who rates a sister for some needless fear,
And in each youth beholds a hero near.
There is—though why proceed through womankind—
In whom ideal loveliness we find.
But while we say within a soul so clad
An instance of this union may be had,
Not the less real because fools deny
That Heav'n to clay can ever be so nigh,
So intimately join'd as to produce
A perfect image for our present use—
There still lies all around them for their feet
A ground where Heav'n and earth can closely meet.
Where earthly pleasures wait upon their hours
Enhanced divinely, as in Eden's bowers,
More than e'er Phædra contemplated when
She said "that various were the joys for men;"
For there is here an earth already new
Found realized and present to the view,
By those aye in Heav'n while below they stray,
And feel the glow of its supernal ray,

Who find in sorrow, sprightliness, or prayer,
That, clad in flesh, they still themselves are there,
Enjoying happiness with all who see
Such rays of beauty and felicity.
Yes, not to Poets only is the way,
Or to Musicians open, as did say
Beethoven, by the aid of Beauty's eyes
To reap on earth a joy that never dies,
To reach that immaterial glorious sphere
Where all we love on earth will be more near—
Where ever these whom Genius did inspire
Will, singing, lead us upwards ever higher,
With us to play and problems e'en propound,
To which the answers in such eyes are found.
Oh, that all artists would this comprehend,
And turn their genius to a glorious end!
Like Raphael, Signole, Herbert, in our day,
They'd show no more mere perishable clay;
Inspired by this light, the light of Truth,
They'd show us real woman, in her youth,
Immortal as the goodness whose soft nest
Lies in the faith and honour of her breast,
The flesh itself, as first created, pure,
Which is through endless ages to endure.
For passions, now a raiment for the soul,
Are given by Him who made and loved the whole;
And though on earth alone their light may shine,
They even here obstruct not the Divine,
When pure Imagination lights the fire
Which will their potent ministry inspire;

For while proud dulness seeks them to subdue,
Unselfish feeling will their grace renew.
Prévost, malign'd, was not so wholly wrong;
And other Manons might survive in song;
Such wondrous springs in human hearts are found
When earth's lost victims deem'd, in Heav'n are crown'd.
But now, to change the scene, let us demand
What other passes show the happy land.
 Then daily observation yields
 A foretaste of Elysian fields.
 You think the couplet false, or trite?
 'Tis you who have no heart or sight;
 For when you see the just and fair,
 The fault is yours, if you're not there.
 I've seen a people, manly, free,
 Averse from causing misery;
 Averse from war, seditious brawls,
 Aye speeding to where duty calls;
 Ne'er consciously betraying truth,
 While fair, like Heaven's unarm'd youth,
 Pleasant, good-humour'd, frank, and bold,
 And natural both young and old;
 Not deeply taught, I own, and must,
 But never knowingly unjust
 To God, or man, but acting still
 As prompted by an honest will;
 Not calculating future good,
 But simple duty understood;

Who, like great Masinissa King [1],
Might plead that they omit each thing,
Or else commit it simply so—
For why? they nothing better know.
Through ignorance their ill is done,
As when the Temple's spoils were won;
And, like him, would they make amends,
And be of God and angels friends,
If only you would teach them how
Thus to fulfil their silent vow.
For never do they vent the jest
Which Dionysius deem'd the best [2];
They leave that to the pedants grave,
Who ancient truths for riches brave.
Their faults by long past men were sown;
Their virtues now are all their own;
Never ill-natured and unfair,
As testifies the face they wear:
True ants and bees for industry,
With order-loving liberty,
With whom each wight may pass his life
And never have a moment's strife,
Or e'en receive an unkind look,
Or meet with any thing to brook—
Men who, for one small act or word,
Caress you as a singing-bird;
In short, a multitude all kind,
Of simple and contented mind—

---

[1] Val. Max. lib. i. 3.   [2] Ibid.

A family of millions near,
To whose deep heart what's right is dear.
Now to have seen this once should be
A lasting store for memory,
Though the next morrow all should blot,
As if it had existed not.
It proves how Nature, follow'd so,
Can peace on human kind bestow;
And peace, if not Elysium quite,
At least ne'er finds it out of sight.

Then if you will but condescend
To smallest items to attend,
No day can pass without some sign
Of being near what is Divine
In common life, where what you see
Can with the angel-life agree.
If but the good will seek the good,
Then this is quickly understood.
I sing for those who may be said
To have within them as is read
Of bright Laconia, temples wall'd,
Minerva Keleutheia call'd;
Since on each road and path are seen
By all such wise observers keen,
The products of that gracious plan
Which God laid down on earth for man;
As erst, while walking thus, Mozart
Found time and subjects for his art,

Could gracious melodies compose,
To yield us joy or heal our woes.
I sing not for men stately, grave,
Who think appearances to save
By scorning logic of the heart,
Which all their talent can't impart.
Cite childish instances for proof,
And they from you will stand aloof;
But 'tis not these that I address,
And so I venture to express
The thoughts which float within the mind
Of those whom Pride can never blind.
So, undismay'd, I pass along,
And turn whate'er I see to song,
As if what is most common here
Denotes the land to which we're near.
The playful boys that children tend,
And on them their prized sweets expend,
Proofs of unconscious human love,
Seem copies rude of what's above.
Not strange, since even birds can show,
What Heav'n has will'd they should bestow.
The youth who has such valour high
To save from danger some one nigh;
The man who strength and skill employs
To seize some wretch that life destroys;
The gentle answer and the smile
That stranger's sorrow will beguile;
The soul, in roughest vesture clad,
That shields the woman or the lad;

The children who in groups will sit
And revel in their feasts of wit;
The heart of Annie bound " to mother,"
Which keeps a corner for another;
The beauteous Lizzie, loving home,
Who cares not from it oft to roam;
The lads that saunter forth to play,
Such friends upon a holiday!
The charities of life so great,
So visible in every state—
These sights familiar at each hour
Possess, at times, a secret power
To plunge the mind in contemplation
Of what surpasses admiration;
Yea, even of that life above
Where all is brightness, rapture, love;
And even they display it here,
As if already it were near,
Conjoin'd with all that now we see
In one supreme felicity.
Attention only is required,
This union then must be admired,
At which I now but cast a glance,
Mark'd fuller as we shall advance.

But here another common passage shows,
Through which a certain stream of Eden flows,
More plainly still the origin of mirth,
Which, like the sunbeams can rejoice the earth.

CANTO IV.

BY MIRTH.

O DARK illusions sad!
That would fair forms and colours bright efface,
So gay in Nature's face,
And sombre hues diffuse that mark the bad,
As in snakes, noxious all,
That never wear a tint to please the eye—
Avaunt! far from us fly,
With all thy code of dull and formal rules
For ceremonious fools:
It is not thou that canst bless'd Fields forestall.
But sing we now that charming mirth
Which can unite those meads with earth,
Comprising e'en the lowest thing
To which its way the heart can wing.

There are more smiles than gloomy frowns in life,
Though fraught, alas! too oft with angry strife;
For whatsoever sometimes comes in sight,
Man still is prompt to hail with joy, Delight;
According to his nature's primal bent,
Which only proves what his Creator meant.
Yet on a disunited earth is found
For lively, constant joy but scanty ground.
Pliny thus says of one whose mien was gay,
" Right cheerful was he, or, at least, I'd say,

Like to a cheerful man, which is as great,
If the true worth of human things you'd rate."
By earth disjoin'd, and separated so
From Heaven, as we tread all ways below,
We mean that world which by itself is view'd
Alone; and, sooth, that needs to be renew'd,
Which Spenser in two words does grandly teach,
If we their depth and whole extension reach.
For faithless Sansfoy he proclaims the sire
Of joyless Sansjoy, whom we can't admire.
"The creature still is good," says Isidore,
"But mutable." He pauses—says no more.
Then who, on such an earth may be quite free
From mental sorrows, causing misery?
For with cupidities still burning ever,
There may be riches, glory,—pleasures never.
Then, as we read, "the earth will grieve each eye,
And all its verdant herbage will grow dry;
The midday sun falls joyless on the hills,
And dust is what you find in dried-up rills."
Connect once more with Heaven such an earth,
And flow'ry meads will yield all mankind mirth.
Each bosom's lord sits lightly on his throne,
And will an unaccustom'd spirit own;
With cheerful thoughts he's lifted from the ground,
And Eden's garden here on earth is found.
For God walks with him on his cheerful way,
And he for all he feels a grace will say;
For what he has received from the least thing
Grace from his heart he audibly will sing;

Whether it be for what some page has wrought
In his own mind, or for spontaneous thought,
For Beauty or for music passing by,
For all he sees and hears that brings joy nigh ;
For a sweet friendly word, a look, a smile,
A stroll at evening that can time beguile ;
For the pale moonlight or the sun's bright ray ;
For what by chance he finds upon his way,
As when the book that suits him meets his eye,
And " Providence of books " seems to imply ;
For all the joys that lighten up his heart
Grace will he say which will fresh joy impart.
His instincts become pure, to good direct,
As if nought more were left him to expect.
O'er floods of light will swim his buoyant soul,
Divinity seems pour'd upon the whole.
But though his " grace " is audible, he feels
It never yet his pleasures deep reveals ;
He would create a language all of fire,
To sing what God and Nature will inspire.

Perhaps by some his visions are deem'd mad,
But still he cries, assured of being glad,
O brilliant air, immense, transparent, high,
Resound with cries of joy to which I fly !
It is that Heav'n, though veil'd, has met his view,
And so for him the earth itself is new.

This joy comes down to us at times from far,
As when we gaze upon the evening star,
The early dawn, the landscape growing bright,
Some striking, beauteous play of shade and light;
But oftener it floats to us on wings
Composed of small, unutterable things,
Suggested by some object, or some sound,
Some ray or colour on the chequer'd ground—
What Homer calls " a good companion " wind,
Such as oft o'er the purple heath we find,
For which the ancients would two heifers white
Insanely kill, to gain that sweet delight,
While Zephyrs without sacrifices yield
To us the air of the Elysian field—
A blade of grass, soft moss, a sun-lit spot,
A transient sight of what is ne'er forgot,
A brook, a slope, a flower, or a weed,
Some object on which memory can feed,
Some tender tint that ravishes the eye,
At sundry bright hours in the summer's sky,
Or, what is more, a word, a look, an air,
So well-named thus, when some you love are there—
'Tis nothing, yet 'tis every thing and all,
Nameless, infinitessimally small;—
It comes to us in things that will defy
Reason, for which no food it will supply.
Admitting of no rule or measure, they
Prove wise the servant who this rule did say,
E'en wiser than his master for the thought
That Reason in such things should ne'er be sought;

Although the ancients by their means, could fly
And even, as they said, could reach the sky,
So as to touch their Jupiter's high throne,
The noblest words for bliss supreme then known.
This joy is quickly said, but not defined;
Mysterious is its action on the mind.
It never lasts, 'tis true; when come, 'tis gone;
But in that moment more by man is won
Than all the kingdoms of the earth could grant,
For which ambitious earthly fools will pant.
No words can e'er describe its potent sway,
Unrivall'd as it is from day to day.
No science analytical can show
Its composition. Nothing more we know
Than this, that, for an instant felt by us,
It comes into our souls enchanted thus.
I thence conclude that it is Heav'n on earth—
A moment's foretaste of th' Eternal mirth.

'Tis fears and doubts that blind men to this good,
And cause e'en no joys to be understood.
That Heav'n is near to earth men will not believe,
They think earth's pleasures only can deceive;
It seems to them that here they ever must
Be wrongful feelings that we should not trust,
Too clearly offspring of the earth and time,
To be connected with another clime;
They think them coarse, and not what they call pure,
While all that flows from Heaven is demure,

As they conceive; though from that azure hill
There bubbles down of mirth a wildish rill,
Where all are solaced, and at times can play
Sequester'd far from each grave formal way.
The sage seems here to bear him like the fop
Whose mirth at all that's natural will stop;
Too delicate by half even to touch
What would disgust his grandeur overmuch;
Too fine to hold that roses should be smelt,
Or silky moss as soft as down be felt.
He thinks he's right because he can't explain
What he would scorn or shudder to ordain.
Nothing attracts him but what he calls nice—
Kid gloves or Tokay, marmalade or ice.
A pale discolour'd air before him floats,
He hates all smiling, and on nothing dotes.
But gloom, much more than brightness, can beguile;
And talk like his is but the earthly style.
Formality and sullens may be grand,
But both are natives of this lowest land.
The grandeur is fictitious at the best,
And out of harmony with all the rest.
Dame Nature has come from Heav'n, as we know,
And gay, light fashions she is sure to show.
She has some whims and measures of her own
Whereby her taste for mirth is plainly shown:
Fashions we'd think that needs must interfere
With some strict notions about mirth found here.

Nor is she very nice in choice of place,
When with a merry heart she would keep pace.
She wants to make us like herself, and see
We'd caught her fashion, and like her were free;
Not like some foolish persons in a town,
Who nought enjoy if ever placed low down.
Whereas high spirits and a joyous heart
Can laugh the same, take all things in good part.
Indeed, 'twere hard to say how she could tell
In plainer language that our mirth is well:
Mirth, not the noisy laughter of a fool,
But quiet, inward, with a surface cool—
Wearing a sweet and loving, serious air,
The most removed from all things that should scare.
It is not conscience makes us cowards all,
But abject doubt which rational we call.
As if sound reason ever could suggest
That Nature's object was not always best.
Yes, life has pleasures manifold and sweet,
In which the earth and fields Elysian meet;
If only man will see the bounds of each,
And the sweet end that kind Heav'n wishes, reach.
For Heaven is joy; to you the words seem trite,
But here they're needed to view all aright.
For since the joys of earth are not the same,
Some think these latter they've a right to blame;

And, even without reference to earth,
There are who doubt and will mistrust all mirth;
As if the joyful laughter of the young
From the Sardinian root called Aches sprung,
That poison'd root, of which the eaters died
Laughing, and hence the phrase diffused so wide
By Homer, who " Sardonic laughter " calls
That which when heard but startles and appals.
Not so grave Anselm, and the high bright school,
When to be joyful here became the rule.
" Joy there," saith he, " shall be without, within,
As if for ever it did first begin ;
Joy will be round about, below, above,
One ocean boundless of Eternal love ;"
And e'en while yet on earth it is the same
As when Jerusalem the text does name,
" An exultation, and her people joy "—
Mysterious words the prophet does employ,
As if these both were now transformëd so,
To be the thing itself while here below.
Therefore e'en those who secretly belong
To that same city verify the song.
Though often with their joy they seem half vex'd ;
And e'en with what flows from Heav'n but perplex'd.
But how are Heav'n and earth conjoined ? you ask.
To answer briefly now becomes the task.
" To find them," says Sarasa, " is an art ;"
With which he then proceeds to inspire the heart.
Although in truth less learned people find
The art he speaks of in their simple mind;

F

While oft tradition in the days of yore,
Did yield to heathens somewhat of its store:
For never were they gay when they opposed
What was by them the purest truth supposed.
Still "joy," he says, "by art, not nature found,
Is ne'er fortuitous when truly sound,
Nor merely accidental in its rise—
'Tis learning's fruit which mirthful makes the wise;"
For Eden's sources are joy's only spring,
And these are reach'd by art of which I sing.
Saith he, You must receive the world's true light,
Without which all around the soul is night.
What is that light, Lux Mundi? would you know?
It is that light which never sets below,
Beneath whose radiant beams will fly away
The dark, sad phantoms through which many stray,
As anti-human superstitious fears
So oft the cause of woe and secret tears,
And cruelty, intolerance, and pride,
Which from the soul must both God and Heav'n hide,
Amerced by clouds from all true gladness here,
And left with nought besides around it clear.
"So merry will I be still as I may,"
Says Euphues, "but as thou meanest—nay;"
Although hereafter I might be as you;
Since mirth for me can only be the true.

Oh, what an easy art which all can learn—
To love, and b'leive, and cast off manners stern!
This joy will issue from faith's cloudless sky,
Of which some points we mark while passing by.
Thus love and union constitute for mind
A field through which the streams of Eden wind;
And here, thus passing, be it understood
How Heav'n's great Lord is not more wise than good.
Love is its own reward; yet for that prize
Reward is given, which may well surprise;
And union bathes in beatific light
The smallest acts of man that come in sight.
Oh! pleasant and delightful are these ways,
And yet 'tis them that Paradise repays!
And then humility—how sweet that dell!
As those who pluck its flow'rets ever tell.
What vast horizons from that shelter'd glade!
What fragrance as from violets in shade!
Hid from the cold censorious world deep there,
Like some wild creature in its mossy lair,
You feel a transport that you cannot tell,
While nature whispers—fear not, all is well.
Humility and mirth are comrades free,
That will, and must, for ever here agree;
For charms unearthly wait on every sense,
When all things are enjoy'd without pretence.
Pretence is able to untune the spheres,
And in its presence beauty disappears;

With it encumber'd, men can no more see
Or hear what fills with rapture you and me,
Who in all sounds of music heard around,
And in all works of art have ever found
Some stream, some ray, some thought supremely high
From glorious regions far beyond the sky.
The ancients thought for joy, that guests should be
In number not exceeding nine or three;
Beginning from the last, the Graces then
Would pour Ambrosia for the feast of men,
And adding six, the number would be found
To make the earth a true Elysian ground:
For then the Muses would assist with you,
And all things noble, gracious, come to view.
Then neither would dull silence be found there
Nor sheer loquacity to taint the air;
No tortuous or anxious things would spoil
Their pleasures with a loud and vain turmoil;
But true amenity, with use as well,
Would clothe the words of those who aught would tell.
Gay things of pleasant, daily, common life
Would reign, instead of noisy, vulgar strife.
No snatching would there be, as if in jest
To keep in earnest; for the joy would rest.
But Mirth, so train'd, can have no other end,
Unless to guide you whither all should wend,
To those bless'd fields which no distractions know,
Arresting steps where brightest flowers grow—

Where nought of self-created misery
Can interupt the true felicity
Of minds in which such joy will ever rise,
Though still on earth, symphonious with the skies.

Then, too, in bright Religion's holy rites
On earth are more than all the earth's delights.
This stream of people, jocund, fearless, frank,
From blooming heights and azure mountains sank,
To wind, as now you see, through this life's field,
All wholesome healing things of mirth to yield.
So when in veil'd mystic form God does pass,
The sight all common praises must surpass;
For when God's order reigns within our minds;
To earth alone nought human pleasure binds;
The hamlet, or the city, bright with thought,
Display then here the bliss all hearts have sought,
Bright, not with marble towers, sculptured stones,
But with unearthly gems, that sweet Heav'n owns.
Processions such of course may be denied,
But all Heav'n's grace alike may be defied.
Yet, mark! 'tis human joys I here admire,
Religious later must employ my lyre,
Though vainly, doubtless, then will be its sound,
Since those in songs of earth cannot be found.
But still already think on what we see!
What mirth! what rapture, and felicity!

What's highest and what's lowest join'd in one,
Distrust and superstition wholly gone!
Yes, even here, how much is thus express'd,
Though nothing may be outwardly profess'd.
It is as if, while carelessly we roam,
Of all right glad on earth we find the home.
Here seems perpetual spring, and every fruit
That autumn yields each human taste to suit;
Here is the far-famed Nectar, fount of youth,
And what I'd call " the primrose way of truth."

But would you see the man who journey'd on,
With this mysterious union wholly won?
Natives of Heav'n, cannot be our theme,
Whose lives on earth to many seem a dream.
Pacomius, Romuald, or Theonas
I cite not, mark'd with gladness as they pass,
Nor yet De Sales, nor Jane de Chantal gay,
While haunting all the unfrequented way;
For these are canonized; and only here
The common life of mankind must appear.
Take Mantua's Baptist, liegeman of the Muse,
What joyful accents does he always choose!
Or Lewis of Cornaro would I show,
Whose portrait by himself so many know;
Breathing that final and right joyous cry,
As bathed on earth in pleasures of the sky,
" O friend, how beautiful is life to me!
And, oh, how happy will its last breath be!"

But from these heights of joy let us descend
To lower walks, on which it will attend.
For sports and recreations never jar
With true beatitude espied from far;
Though magistrates right grave of Middlesex
May all within their local power vex,
And think the poor and all, content should be,
With raving speeches for democracy,
Cold with the lions in Trafalgar Square;
But dance in gardens they must never dare.
Public diversions were enjoin'd by saints,
Of whom of old were never heard complaints;
As when Urseolo a third part spent
Of his revenues, and with that intent;
Or as Pope Innocent the Third, so grave,
Did love to see the people play and rave
Upon a holiday with honest glee,
Contented, innocent, in gladness free;
Or as the whole of London, in days past,
Where, even yet, true pleasures seem to last—
So hard it is for sophists to efface
The smiles that once lit England's simple face!
'Twas quaintly said of old "The goose is blind,
Which at the fox's sermon you will find;"
And so perhaps you will mistrust the wight
Who you to mirth and dancing will invite.
Yet, say whate'er you will, one fact is plain,
That mirth to man will come, and not in vain.
Yes, weeping, wailing, are not every day,
And oft men's faces prove the fact I say.

The song itself must playful be,
　As if it skipp'd from trammels free.
How many pairs of friends who walk,
And laughing, smiling, ever talk,
Each soul, as in a crystal shrine,
Seen through that sheath or veil to shine.
You'd think upon their happy way
'Twas through Elysium they did stray.
But moments spent in smiling so
A true mysterious joy bestow—
Mysterious, if you will but think,
And to the roots of things will sink.
Observe the lips, the arm, the eye,
And this is what you can't deny;
For the bright face that each will wear
Denotes how more than earth is there;
How immaterial is the spring
Which brings to sight each joyous thing!
Even those who see them smile
Feel almost in Heav'n the while,
And are forced to smile themselves,
As if by some fairy elves:
For such mirth is like a spell
That can cure and make all well.
But, mark! I sing for those who see
What formal fools say cannot be.
Yet 'tis so true, that writers grave,
Intent on men to guide and save,
Like Nieremberg e'en so austere,
And, we may add, so oft severe,

Seems forced, on seeing it, to own
That faces thus reflect Heav'n's tone
Even when thus expressing mirth,
Or any common joy of earth;
And his conclusion from the fact
That faces can denote the act
Of daily goodness bringing joy,
Is that same image to employ
To prove the beatific vision
Will change our bodies, with addition
Of a new outward brightness so
Surpassing all that's fair below.
Then the dance, with mirthful tunes,
Puts to flight all morbid lunes.
Pride, dark Pride will never dance;
Not for him that sweetest trance:
Such the law of Nature—seen
In our daily life, I ween;
Banish him, and you will see
Twinkling feet will skip with glee—
Not as in the German round,
Where scarce movement heeds the sound,
But as in the airy flight,
All the graces within sight,
Such as music can inspire,
Of which eyes can never tire,
The country-dance, or gay quadrille,
Which with such joy the heart can fill.
Yes, this dance-music, quite alone,
Seems to re-echo Heav'n's sweet tone:

At least it raises up our hearts
And an ideal life imparts,
Making us rave of higher mirth—
A happiness not of this earth;
Though the dark sophists who now reign
Of that quick sound will oft complain,
As thinking it cannot agree
With a bright Sunday's pleasures free.
Let Pride be absent, and you'll find
The very stones to you are kind;
Although as in some foreign street
They may not suit your London feet,
Of which the boots will seem to be
Like what's described in history—
Those fairy slippers made of glass,
Which well became the sweet meek lass;
While here, indeed, I promise you
Our girls soon find they'd never do;
As may be witnessed by the wag,
Who sees them skip from crag to crag:
Heedless of grace the strain may lend,
Obliged to use the Grecian bend.
Or haste now to the ocean shore,
Where Mirth will often frolic more;
Haste to the diamond-sparkling sand,
Where Pouliguen frequents the strand;
The noblest maidens bare-foot there
To make the swell that meets them stare;
As paddling through transparent brine
Their tiny limbs like Nereids' shine,

In innocence their pure hearts bathed
And Pride's "appearances" all braved,
Till evening will renew their glee,
And joy attains its apogee
In Music's strain, most soft on high,
And Heav'n is felt by all as nigh.
Then look at Mirth when sparkling round,
And in some great assembly found,
Not as seen, oft between two,
Playing just like me and you.
Laughter of a common crowd
Rings with what we say aloud;
No disagreement or dissent;
All from a better clime is sent:
For joy and union, when combined
With innocence, you there can find,
And nations, who refuse that gift
Through sorrows only raving drift;
Though by their nature apt for mirth,
They cannot reap it from the earth,
When link'd with errors, as in France,
When men reject sweet Heav'n's advance;
The Gallic sophist's murky school
Does true heart's gaiety so cool.
That mirth from Heav'n thus is sent
Seems clear, it is so innocent,
So natural, from errors free,
With which it never can agree;
For wheresoever it is found,
Society is safe and sound.

Ah! do indulge me, let me sing
Of each fair, sprightly, heav'nly thing!
Mirth's acme acted can combine
With what in maidens is divine.
Then suffer them to have their glee,
Though but put on for you and me.
Its sweet ideal is so pure,
Though it may never long endure!
So easily, with innocence,
Enjoy'd it is without pretence!
Sober nature has a way
Simple still, however gay.
Mark the bright Nymph who leaves the stage,
How instantly becoming sage,
When from the scene she scarce has pass'd,
And sung, or danced, or skipp'd her last!
Some side observers can perceive
How soon she will her Nymphship leave,
Doffing all airs that throng to please,
Resuming her sweet wonted ease,
So carelessly she walks away,
Perhaps still warbling her lay,
And drawing from their souls a prayer,
That her may Heav'n's joy follow there.

And why not? say thou bigot cold,
When Bacon, wisest of our fold,
Maintains that skipping, dancing so
Can innate science even show,

Conferring still complete delight
By hearing, and not less by sight,
A joy confined to no degree,
To all men here felicity?
But hear his very words again,
As if a mediæval strain,
"Music has pleasures that flow from the visible,
Witness the dancers, and see how 'tis credible,
Though no such posturing ere can be audible,
Yet then both are more lovable.
'Tis not the ear only that must be satisfied,
If by the music you would be most gratified;
For by the sound must the movements be rectified
And suiting gestures multiplied.
But when the ears and the eye are both ban-
    queted,
Then is the charm of music quite perfected,
And to the twofold enchantment all subjected,
And this has Mirth ne'er rejected[1]."

Well, in the fields it is the same:
Where Mirth from wise men hears no blame.
The Grecian muse did sing
What crowns me there a king.
Oh, let me then, I pray,
Be mirthful as I may.
I will, I will be mad!
Alcmeon madness had;

[1] Opus Tertium, cap. 58, &c.

Orestes was the same,
Whose white feet poets name;
They both their mothers slew,
If what we hear is true.
But I would no one slay;
I nothing would but play;
I feel so wildly glad,
I will, I will be mad!
Mad, too, was Hercules,
And in ferocious ways,
With arrows darted low,
From Iphiteon bow.
Great Ajax, too, was mad,
While wielding, gloomy, sad.
The sword of Hector fell,
With direful shield as well.
But I, who hold a flower,
No bow, no sword to lour,
Must now, and will be mad!
With mirth I am so glad.

So it was in days of old,
As in Paris we behold,
When the " Pré-aux-Clercs " was screen'd
'Gainst all foes that intervened,
From e'en monks, or worse, the King[1],
Who would cut the student's wing,
Not merely " martinets," but those
Who to be real scholars chose.

[1] See Crevier's Hist. de l'Université de Paris, tom. vi. passim.

CANTO IV.

That meadow with its dauntless boys
Did lead through sport to distant joys,
Just as with us the stream and field
Can the same kind of rapture yield;
For gladness, whene'er found, must be
A rill from Heav'n's felicity.
And yet how often did men try
To oust the University
From all that honest recreation
Provided there for every nation!
With us 'tis still those scholars cry;
For " to enclose it we defy
All builders, governments, and squires,"
Though soon with us each champion tires,
Frustrated, compell'd to suffer,
And not e'en complaints to utter.
But mirth with wisdom then prevail'd,
And so that ground was uncurtail'd.
" A learned man should never choose,"
Says Seneca, " his arms to use;"
" It is indecent," then he adds,
" That he should play like common lads."
Our masters of a former day
Would never heed what such men say:
And so to save the field for ever
Was still their constant, firm endeavour,
E'en aided by the Holy See,
That would protect the students' glee;
Both scholars and professors knew
What visions they had in their view,

As often as they sported free
And gladden'd poor humanity.

But now return we to the street,
And there watch closely all we meet.
What play, what tricks, good-natured fun!
In hearts there is a noon-day sun.
And small disasters even cause
A laugh which chimes with Heav'n's own laws.
For doubtless angels oft beguile
Celestial mirth with such a smile;
Since all from charity it flows,
Which makes us often thus suppose
What we ourselves would like to hear
From those who to our hearts are dear.
Then let us too observe the slang
Which on the highways often rang,
Having good-humour for its food
When 'tis rightly understood;
For know that I would have you learn,
It is with depths it has concern,
Not with the surface so exact,
Which is a right curious fact.
The soul when flush'd with joy and mirth
Will skim or soar above this earth;
And all mere pride it will disdain,
And e'en of the correct complain
While its free, wild, unguarded speech
Can heights beyond the haughty reach.

In truth, it is from Heav'n comes down
Mirth to the country and the town.
You say 'tis animal. E'en so;
From God no less the joy must flow.
A dull, vain stamp it never bears,
And so far Heav'n's own bright mark wears;
Besides we are Athenians then,
When talking thus like common men—
E'en Lysias' disciples, whose
Fine sentences can no word lose
Without the loss of sense as well,
As Favorinus marks to tell,
Contrasting his with Plato's way,
Many of whose sweet words you may
Omit without the loss of sense,
Though injured be its elegance [1].
Those Greeks detested speeches long,
And deem'd that many words were wrong;
In fewest all their thoughts to say
Appear'd to them the wisest way.
Of orators the most concise
Was Phocion, ever yet precise.
So once, before to speak he rose,
His eyes, as thinking, he must close,
Appearing wholly lost in thought—
To tell the cause he was besought.

---

[1] Aul. Gel. book ii.

"I'm thinking then," he did reply,
"If you will ask the reason why,
Meditating all this while
How I can abridge my style."
Now here one word of slang effects
What this great orator expects;
So that its phrases, quaint and short,
By questions, or a sly retort,
Seem to accomplish the same end
For which he would his wisdom spend.
 In English fun, the French would show,
'Tis oft the style of Marivaux;
The playful use of words can prove
A sign of being what you love.
If all this you refuse to see,
I'd say adopt vulgarity;
Just as Gavarni once did say,
Adopting a fine poet's way,
Unto his lady-love refined
Who his bright thoughts had not divined,
"Mary, what you want, I swear,
Is that you should ever wear
Somewhat that I would express
As a coarse, more vulgar dress
In your looks, and in your talk,
When you sit, or ride, or walk."
But this, forsooth, is wand'ring far
From money, now the only star
Of gaiety as it is thought,
Even when joy's expressly sought.

And then again, a graver cause
Thus to such mirth a wise heart draws;
Though some men, learnëd more than wise,
May all its pleasantry despise.
E'en facetiousness is thought
In the wise to be a fault;
Therefore Cicero takes care
Scævola should not be there
When he cites some happy jest
Which appear'd to him the best;
So, though present at the first
Dialogues, he never durst
Show him enter'd when the theme
To grow pleasanter might seem,
Thinking that a man so grave
Should appearances thus save;
For the ancients aye observed
Rules from which they never swerved.
Mirth seem'd unbecoming here,
If the Pontiff should appear.
Yet these same old Romans oft
Stately airs and language doft.
Horace with Mecænas jests,
Merrily the fact attests:
" While 'tis thought that we converse
On state secrets, the reverse,"
Said he, " does bespeak our style,
When oft sweet hours we beguile,
Talking but of this and that,
With some right familiar chat

About sunshine or the rain,
When of weather we complain,
Urging fineness of the day,
Being all we have to say."
So, parenthetically, here
We English not so strange appear,
Since Horace and Mæcænas thus
Did daily talk, like each of us;
Which, after all, is wiser far
Than seeking public peace to mar
By talk seditious, as in France,
Where party-babble all advance,
Until at last a war must be
The climax of felicity,
When journalists, who faith defend,
Shout like the rest, and genius spend
To sanction battles, and to show
How military arts they know;
While those whom they disgust, surprise,
They villify and stigmatize.
Nathless, while these such views deplore,
They only value joy the more.
'Tis mirth, moreover, that escapes
From all proud controversial shapes,
That come like Harpies to destroy
What erst had won our peace and joy.
Oh, then, how oft profoundly wise
Is he who this bland method tries!
For mental pride that ever spins
Its web round truth still nothing wins;

Unless it counts it for a gain
To spend its slime and then complain,
Apostatizing for a word,
Which humble joy deems acts absurd,
While scorning, for its part to pry
Into deep secrets of the sky,
Synthetically fix'd to see
Whate'er can with the truth agree.
Then gaiety itself leads back
Ideas to sweet Nature's track.
So when, in France, the social tone
Seem'd resting on feign'd rules alone,
It is to gaiety were due
The true ideas that men knew,
As well as their expression free
By mirth obliged with truth to be.

In brief, wherever mirth can dwell
In real brightness much is well.
Joy favours love and union blest;
Grief deems displeasure must be best,
In language finding thus a word
Which proves maligning joy absurd.
The earth, through joy, oft reaches then
To the true home prepared for men.

But, say, how know we joy is there,
With such grim facts so oft to scare
Those who will view the whole of life,
Where oft all nature seems but strife?

And then such clever men contend
That joy, protracted without end,
Involves a base, unworthy thought
Of what in mind should ne'er be sought!
These last, forsooth, appear to me
Like men whom long obscurity
Of some dark, painful dungeon cell
Makes them suppose that nought is well
But chequer'd shade, with scarcely light,
Which if increased would wound their sight.
I hold their view of what should please
To indicate some mere disease;
As when to jaundiced eyes appear
Discolour'd things most bright and clear.
I leave them, to pursue my task
To answer others what they ask,
When doubting elsewhere there can be
What we call joy and ecstasy.
The proofs abound, if only we
Will ponder on the facts we see.
For joy must be the good supreme,
When woke up from the grim world's dream.
In God's own likeness we are told
Our race was made. But we behold
In youth and childhood, fresh from Him,
How joy and mirth o'erflow the brim
Of their sweet, pure intelligence,
Which we conclude derives them thence.
For man may sin, and gloomy grow;
But not from Him does sadness flow.

'Tis man who makes a grumbling world,
As through his fancies he is whirl'd.
'Tis he makes all false gravity,
Opposing true hilarity.

Man's joy, I grant, implieth health;
But whence to him will flow joy's wealth?
From organs, humours, dost thou say?
But without joy they yet can play
Their part; and yet deep gloom may shed
Its sable vesture round his head.
The secret, then, of joy is still
Mysterious, try howe'er you will.
The whole and sole fact that we know,
Is that it was intended so.
The analyzer then is left
Of other inference bereft.
But joy, since God wills joy, must be
A wine from lands we do not see;
For earth and matter have no spring
From which can rise so pure a thing,
Whose charm must therefore emanate
First from another higher state.
What sparkles in that heart of thine
Comes pure from Paradise's vine!

True mirth, we find, can never be
Combined with incredulity.

Voltaire took pains on her to call;
With what success is known to all.
The comic Muse refused his prayer,
And failure palpable was there.
The revolutionary school
Has sad austerity for rule;
No smiles are seen upon its face;
A savage gloom is all its trace.
Pride can be tragic, stately, high:
He ne'er attains hilarity;
Which proves that from another land
Descends true joy with manners bland.
What we call gaiety is thus
A mystery that lasts for us;
Since analyze it no one can;
Reflecting on it's vain for man.
This gift is yours to-day 'tis plain
But will it e'er be yours again?
No one can tell if 'twill come back,
Or e'er can calculate its track.
No path exists to guide you there,
No source beneath this earth's bright air
From which you can be sure to draw
This spirit seeming without law.
So, knowing not its course or fount,
But only its effect's amount,
The gravest thinkers all allow
It comes to us we know not how.
Whence they conclude 'tis inspiration
More than what causes admiration,

That high enthusiastic turn,
When minds exalted brightest burn.
So we infer that 'tis a ray
From Heav'n that shines upon our way.

But lower creatures let us take,
And of their ways an instance make,
Not pressing on your simple bard
Exceptions which are sometimes hard,
Who would dismiss them when he can,
As not God's likeness, as in man.
But showing gladness in the small
'Gainst joy's high fount's no proof at all.

The bliss pervading all these creatures here
To an observant eye makes Nature dear.
For them the air, the water, and the ground,
With joys congenial constantly abound;
Which proves whatever forms He did employ,
That He who made them meant them to have joy.
So joy supreme must elsewhere be the law
Of that great source whence they existence draw;
And what opposes joy without grave cause,
Opposes, so far, the eternal laws.
Each rural home presents a varied page,
Deserving study by the deepest sage.

Its living creatures, whether wild or tame,
Denote by joy so clearly whence they came;
And e'en to watch their ways can always yield
An entrance open to our first bright field,
Where animals did ever roam with glee
Round Adam, like him, innocent and free.
But mark, how even in expression, too,
Their joy resembles what would grace e'en you.
For clearly most of them were meant to play
In their own mirthful, harmless, graceful way.
  A child might interrupt the song,
  Demanding if you deem it wrong.
  From whom can such a truth be hid,
  If watch'd should be the lamb or kid?
  While still with others all their lives
  A corresponding joy survives,
  As in our dogs can witness'd be,
  True types of fun and jollity.
  And then perhaps of these, who knows?
  It may be true, as some suppose,
  That even they may live again,
  And still some other joy retain;
  At least, we read God made not death,
  As Solomon in "Wisdom" saith;
  And death for all, we think, began
  With the mysterious fall of man.
  Though Science inferences draws
  From teeth, and from the form of jaws;
  Which may be rash, for all we know;
  As sometimes Science argues so;

While men as wise, prefer what's writ
To all its anatomic wit.
Still Plutarch seems to go too far,
Whose text with present laws will jar;
But here I flounder in the dark,
As you, no doubt, will soon remark.
Yet think what happiness would rise
From scales descending in the skies!
Even as now we see them here,
Where each inferior is so dear.
If I my fancies might avow,
It may hereafter be as now.
A world organic harmonized
Would e'en in Paradise be prized;
Though lower it should still descend,
And not with human beings end:
But this is hinted by the way,
Nor mean we in such fields to stray.
Still clearly from the whole we see
The thoughts of Heav'n with earth agree,
Diffusing happiness around,
And mirth, as are in creatures found.
If joy was meant for them so low,
What would not Heav'n on man bestow?
Unless you think that joy can be
Proof of inferiority.
Then Heav'n, prescribing all that's fair,
Leads us to think that more is there
Resembling what is found on earth
Than what we fancy here has birth.

Since e'en these lower creatures can
Evince the self-same tastes as man,
Which shows them made by one great Hand,
That wrought more than we understand.
Forgive me if I now relate
An instance, abrogating state.
Two pigeons comely caught my eye,
Both walking on the roadway by ;
Each look'd right sleek and most elate,
As if it loved its cheerful mate ;
When coming to a muddy spot,
Soil their clean feet, sooth, they would not ;
So they just skipp'd across ; when I
Their delicacy did descry—
For they had thus been taught to shun
Defilement ; so my task is done,
To show one Master taught us all,
The high and mighty, and the small.
Thus 'tis not only mirth must be
In Heaven as on earth we see ;
There must be e'en some tastes as well,
Which in ourselves are found to dwell.
Though some of these of course belong
To what in high Heav'n would be wrong.
For, as the buds on trees will wear
A raiment fitted for the air,
In winter glutinous and rude
To make scream out each silly prude,
In spring and summer, all thrown off,
Each will its slimy vesture doff,

So in this present life is given
Some things to man not found in Heav'n;
While even these decorum need
What nature did intend to breed.
Decorum, as we see on earth,
Is link'd above with Heav'n's own mirth;
Its sense and value are so great,
They must be in the future state.
But as for joy, which some reprove,
There it must last supreme above;
For cloudless mirth would ever reign
If there were here no worldly stain,
Such as in Heaven cannot be,
So there lives hilarity,
Joy and mirth, without a sigh,
Or a dull formality;
Therefore joy and bliss on earth
Lead us to where both have birth,
Where for short moments, too, we stray,
As if e'en through Heaven led our way,
Where no sad gravity can dwell—
Though here at times it may be well;
While gravity I still must believe
Springs only from the sin of Eve.
There, none will types from Michoel borrow,
As ladies full of scorn and sorrow
Who scarcely can refrain from tears,
Since nothing tearful there appears
Amid bright scenes that fancy paints,
And where are heard no dull complaints,

For innocent is mirth, and holy,
Therefore celestial is it wholly.

Alas! I fear, too light and vain
Still hitherto has been my strain,
When I reflect on what might sing
Bright angels, other proof to bring.
For spirits most opposed to mirth,
Of all our human joy a dearth,
Were witness'd by our Lord with pain,
When His disciples did complain
Of His departure when announced,
Which they would loudly have denounced.
Said He "Because I go away,
You seem quite sorrowful to-day;
And sadness thus has fill'd your hearts
When hearing that your Lord departs.
But, mark! it is the truth I tell—
My going hence for you is well,
Since to you here We soon will send
The Paraclete, that constant Friend,
Who His sweet presence will employ
By granting you a lasting joy
For ever with you to remain."
So here on earth is Heav'n again;
For who can read, or reading see
Such gracious, great benignity,
And not conclude that gladness thus
Is meant expressly now for us?

O gracious God! to think that Thou
Dost mark the sadness in us now,
Is quite enough to make us feel
That Thou wouldst Heav'n e'en here reveal.

Yes, joy, and joy immense must ever be,
When aught thus of Heav'n clearly comes to thee.
" Serve God with gladness," is the Psalmist's cry ;
" The hearts of those who seek Him never sigh ;"
" Happy the people who, rejoicing know ;
With them while here on earth will gladness flow;"
For " heartfelt joy is the true life of man :
Imagine what is better no one can."
Jerusalem is thus where men rejoice ;
And blameless ever is that happy choice.

But here enough is sung for you to see
How joy on earth joins Heav'n's felicity.
'Tis true, a future, not a present goal
Is here presented to each human soul,
Which hears but this: " A day, a day is near
When all you loved will fresh with joy appear."
But the same holy song proceeds to say,
" With this hope gladden'd, let's pursue the way,"
So gladden'd are still many here, they seem
Already ravish'd by a glorious dream—
Not like Æneas do they show the trace
Of only hope pretended on their face,
Who only could allege " perhaps " for those
Whom he encouraged to support their woes.

If a poor bard profane might venture so,
He'd say of them, that even here below
They have already reach'd that Country true,
That " Patria" still ever in their view,
Of which the name, when sweetly chanted here,
Bedews the eye that would conceal its tear.
  This Earth with sorrow must combine,
  But here all gladness is Divine,
  The radiance of another sphere,
  An unpolluted brightness clear,
  To which by gladness we come near.
  Since mirth can open such a way,
  It is with her that we should stray,
  And leave false gravity to those
  Who are not what the vain suppose.

  But would you hear a mystic proof
  From which great minds stood not aloof?
  Gennadius, Physician sage,
  Appears from Saint Augustine's page,
  As having doubted if there be
  Another life for men to see.
  Having long loved and served the poor,
  Heav'n will'd his doubts should not endure.
  So, it is said, an angel, sent
  From high with that express intent,
  Did lead him in his sleep to hear
  The melodies of Heaven near.
  'Twas through a city that he walk'd,
  And, wondering, with the angel talk'd!

Who told him that th' unearthly sound
In Heav'n's bright mansions floated round,
That thence, descending to his ear,
They reach'd him to dispel his fear.
The doctor woke, and, leaving bed,
" 'Tis but an idle dream," he said.
But on the next succeeding night
The same bright angel came in sight,
And ask'd if him he recognized?
Who answered, " Yes," as not surprised.
" How so?" the youth angelic said.
" 'Twas you," he answer'd, " who me led
To hear the joyful, blissful cry
Of Heav'n's great court above on high."
" Sleeping or waking," then ask'd he,
" Did you so hear this prodigy?"
" While sleeping soundly," he replied.
" 'Twas so; the fact is not denied,"
Answer'd the angel; " but then know,
'Tis sleeping you see Heaven so.
Where is your body now?" ask'd he.
" 'Tis in my chamber sole with thee."
" Know you not that your eyes are closed?
And seeing nought as you supposed?"
" Yes," he replied, " I know it now."
" And yet you see me! tell me how?"
The other spake not. Then the youth
Proceeded to instil the truth.
" As now your eyes yield no effect,
And yet you see, so still expect

HEAVEN ON EARTH.

An operation just the same,
Showing the home from which you came.
Another life can then be yours,
As your experience thus assures ;
With other senses you will feel
That which to you I here reveal."
Now, mark, what saw—what heard he then ?
A youth more fair than sons of men,
A sound more sweet and more sublime
Than ever woke the ear of Time.
Conclude that in Heav'n there is mirth,
There beauty, and all joy have birth,
And also, that when earth is gay,
To Eden near may be your way,
The gate not closed, the entrance found—
The earth becomes a heav'nly ground ;
From joy to joy you pass along,
And verify the lofty song.
Then Mirth ! whom Milton e'en admired,
Who by no baseness can be hired,
Whate'er thou art, do not disdain
Me, or my unpretending strain.
Oh, come and lodge within my bow'r,
And make eternity each hour ;
With simple joys we'll pass the time,
And think we hear old Eden's chime ;
For play I love, and music, books,
Songs, and, above all, thy sweet looks !
The town and country, in short, all—
A gift from sweet Heav'n each I call ;

Yea, even pensive melancholy,
And what appears to pedants, folly.
Come then, sweet Pleasure, to my side,
O faithful comrade, though belied;
For well I know here whence thou fliest
E'en down to me—'tis from the highest
Hills of Paradise up above,
And thou, too, bringest with thee, Love,
Soft Love which feels it sweet to die
Much rather than forswear the sky,
Who with thee e'en will cease to play—
Yea, more, will send thee right away,
Rather than lose thee for the years
Eternal—the sole loss he fears—
So that e'en thou thyself canst be
A guide to true felicity,
While making man a child for ever,
Who thus in all things can find pleasure,
Bearing him back on azure wings
To the sweet garden of which sings
Your Bard, who thus would earth combine
With the sweet land where angels shine;
Leaving all others to complain,
As some did of poor La Fontaine,
That if he had not views profound,
A very fool he would be found;
But since such wit has found the door
Of Paradise, they'll mock no more.
Let's fly the sophists' vaunted sense,
Whose very language is pretence;

Of Paradise we can be birds—
Let's leave to doubting pedants, words.

CANTO V.

BY ADMIRATION (NATURAL OBJECTS).

Another passage here invites our feet,
That leads to grounds where earth and Heav'n will meet;
Or rather, to those true Elysian fields
Where Heav'n its joy, at times, to mankind yields.
The sense of admiration in our race
Produces now this union that we trace;
For Heav'n itself, whate'er it be, would tire,
If spirits there could not, like man, admire.
So admiration in those realms must be
Eternal as their own felicity.
Now the same sense, when exercised below,
Can clearly this great joy of Heav'n bestow;
For when man from his heart feels call'd to praise,
The impulse of itself makes open ways,
Not praising coldly—one mode of disdain
Of which sage Favorinus did complain,
Saying he preferr'd the loudest blame,
As fraught for worthy things with far less shame,
Denoting, as it does, a secret foe,
Than that such scanty praise from lips should flow,

Which seems the language of a real friend
Who vainly tries things worthless to defend.
He adds, what now perhaps is far less clear,
That blame like this falls senseless on the ear
Of those who in such words a foe detect,
And not what they pretend to show, defect.
But each who feels, and noble things will praise,
In that sole act itself through Eden strays.
Enthusiasm blends with earth Heav'n high,
Unites, or makes them to each other nigh;
As the Greek noble word itself can teach,
Defining it as being God in each.
Its sweet delight can minds so much enthral,
That Love, through admiration, lost his all—
His heart, his clothes, his eyes, and so he's blind,
And naked too, as him you ever find.
But still for all these losses what cared he?
Admiring love is such felicity!

What food for admiration here,
With works Divine encircled near!
   The flow'ret of the field,
The face of nature on our way,
Presented to us day by day,
   Which can such wonders yield—

Alas! men now will only scorn.
For Admiration few seem born,
　　Not even earth they see;
But such is not the part for man,
Nor now, nor when he first began,
　　And such it need not be.

Though living now in exile here,
To him is Paradise still near,
　　If nature should inspire
To train his mind to see and love
The things aye close to Heav'n above,
　　Which angels do admire.

Where is the man thus taught to trace
The beauty in all Nature's face,
　　The wonder and the power?
An Eden is the earth to him,
For admiration fills the brim
　　Of mind beneath his bower.

Musing meditation yields
The sweets of Heav'n's Ambrosian fields;
　　The near, no less the far,
Displays the workmanship Divine
Which round, above him still will shine,
　　The flower or the star.

He speaks of mossy seats and wells,
Of grots and valleys bright he tells,
   Of mountain and the lawn,
Of setting suns to fire the cloud,
Of things proclaiming God aloud,
   The dew-lit grass at dawn;

The cypress shades, the violet bank,
The heather, and the rushes dank,
   The lily of the dale,
The verdant leaf to morning spread,
The honeysuckle's fragrant head,
   The rocks he loves to scale;

He speaks of all the greenwood trees,
Of placid lakes and purple seas;
   Around him beauty teems;
He feels a joy no words can tell,
The power of a mighty spell
   Beyond the bliss of dreams.

He speaks of birds that perch and sing,
That seem to understand each thing,
   As if Saint Francis spoke;
The lamb that skips, the dog that bounds,
The charm of song, of music's sounds;
   He feels as if awoke

From a long senseless sleep and bad,
Of inattention, noxious, sad,
   When he could nothing see,
Or even feel as should a man
Created all God's works to scan;
   Such life was not to be.

But now through things more solemn, strange,
He loves, with Science wing'd, to range,
   To wonder at the star;
The distant suns in boundless space,
Those wonders of the spheres to trace;
   His thoughts nought then can bar.

He seems to hear the sphery chime
Of Heaven, his eternal clime,
   To see its glories vast,
To feel that here he still can rise
Beyond all planets in the skies
   Where his true home will last.

No more he even thinks of death,
But as a life, surpassing breath,
   With new and glorious ways;
All gloomy thoughts away are flown,
He feels eternal joys his own,
   And here through heaven he strays.

Just admiration is the joy of man ;
And earth conjoin'd with Heaven is its span ;
It tends to sweeten and exalt our thought,
As if with Eden's fragrance earth were fraught.
And then its absence even can convey
A sign that men are fatally astray
From the bright path, aye mark'd out and design'd
To yield contentment to their heart and mind.
The ludicrous, I find, will now require
Admittance, showing those who can't admire.
But pleasantry exposing what is wrong
Not always is beneath the Muse's song.
And more than all the reasonings of man,
Oft solve some knot, as Horace says, it can ;
As, mixing Chian and Falernian wine,
The flavour of the two you should combine.
No admiration in those circles vain
Where nought is found that can its force sustain.
That poor French Damis well portrays the tribe,
When her past week she will in brief describe
To Pasquin, who had ask'd her to relate
What acts of duty, of importance great,
She had accomplish'd, absent for that space ;
When she consented thus each day to trace :
" You call me, then, of these to give account—
A hundred, say a thousand's the amount.
Sunday, at Monthieu's I was ask'd to dine
With the small Duke and the fat Countess fine.
Monday, a tradesman put me in a fright,
A vile automaton, and unpolite,

Sooth, wanting me to pay him that same day,
Because he too his creditors must pay,
As he pretended ; but I knew the style
Practised by him, and merely to beguile.
On Tuesday, to a man of money I
Went, to cajole, and flattery to try.
On Wednesday I went to the new play :
The world exclaim'd, How fine! but I said nay.
To criticize is one of my pet rules ;
For admiration is the style of fools.
Thursday, I felt a trouble to myself;
I had the spleen, which makes one such an elf !
On Friday, Folly had o'er me full sway ;
Florissa would engross me the whole day.
But yesterday all Paris saw me dress'd
Supremely fine, what cannot be express'd ;
A robe more gorgeous no one ever saw,
Laboutray trimm'd the vest made by Passau.
All eyes were jealous at their sovereign taste—
And here, from leaving them, I come in haste."
Such routine, when protracted through the year,
Makes not the pass to Eden very clear,
At least, by feeling admiration high
For scenery that shows that region nigh.
Here we can see, in fact, but deep defiles—
No doubt a gleam for moments that beguiles,
But this succeeded by thick mists around,
Through which, I fear, no gate of Heav'n is found.

But fly we now unto another pole,
And mark how admiration decks the soul.
Those still amerced, of it may boast their want,
Let's leave them standing there, stripp'd, leafless, gaunt,
And imitate what is of ivy said,
Which ne'er is seen to touch a tree that's dead.
'Tis told in praise of Cicero's great name
That he sought ever to extend the fame
Of all the men of merit of his age;
Such admiration felt the Roman sage
For his contemporaries, thought to be
Well skill'd in speaking or philosophy.
The fame of each he ever did promote
By words of praise, or else by what he wrote.
In brief it seem'd as if he ne'er was tired
Commending those he thought should be admired.
Who sees not quickly, even at a glance,
How such a temper must men's joys enhance?
While those who praise old art but with the view
To vilify, depreciate the new,
Would now have wanted what they vainly praise
Had not the ancients practised other ways.
Now when all living present worth's denied
Of brightest human joy then ebbs the tide.
But hear, what says true Genius from the lips
Of one who golden cups Ambrosian sips:
"The chief great error of my early days
Was in my vein to give but scanty praise;

'Twas not in over-estimating then,
But in too slight esteem for living men,
Acknowledging too faintly merit high;
It is for that I feel I now should sigh."
Most wise complaint, for this, as Bacon said
To contradictions has the best men led,
Opposing good things, when appearing new
To their distorted, partial, feeble view.
Aaron was holy; yet did he oppose
Great Moses, as the sacred volume shows.
When Jerome would translate the sacred text
Men wise and holy felt indignant, vex'd.
When blessed Gregory had pass'd from life
His writings even led to angry strife;
And some, whose hearts towards good did ever turn,
Declared their wish that men his books would burn.
Wise Roger Bacon scruples not to add
That Jews there were, not partners with the bad,
Who when their nation Jesus crucified
Were good themselves, with minds that wander'd wide;
So apt is human poor fragility
Contemporaneous greatness ne'er to see,
To think things present never have a claim
To admiration and eternal fame[1].
But Tacitus remarks it even can
Reveal the deep malignity of man;

[1] Opus Tertium, cap. 9.

When what is ancient only he will praise,
And to commend the present still delays.
Our Ruskin adds, " The spirit most opposed
To admiration has to be exposed."
For Art, he seems to think, can never lead
To those bright fields which we all nathless need—
" Those highest fields," which he confines to Art,
Which can religious truth so well impart,
If men in forms of burlesque take delight,
Connected with the evil of hell's night,
And play thus with the evil of disdain—
Of which, in truth, we often may complain;
As when for entertainment bright and best
The Maid of Orleans becomes a jest,
Each deed heroic shown to folly nigh,
That fools may laugh, and noble spirits sigh.
Though not to recent ages is confined
The fault he blames so hateful to the mind;
For Horace did remonstrate in his day
With those who would at follies only stay—
The higher and the lowest classes both,
To ask for bears and acrobats not loth;
Preferring spectacles, which teach them nought,
To noblest drama with instruction fraught.
There is a burlesque, innocent and gay,
Whatever pedants and grave fools may say,
When we can laugh like children at the show,
Of which the simple foolishness we know.
The worst, as being least pretentious, jest,
Is said by wisest men to be the best.

Mere fable yields a rich, abundant food
For honest mirth, when rightly understood.
The Dragon of Saint George, or Blue Beard cruel,
For playful joy or dread are fittest fuel,
To that will Genius and the people fly,
While senseless Wealth will scorn them passing by,
Vaunting its " comedy genteel," which shows
What ne'er makes joyful him on whom it grows.
But the Burlesque which seizes for its prey
Upon the glories of another day—
Avaunt, the hateful foe of admiration,
Which leaves a cleaving curse on any nation!
Though e'en Cervantes comes in for his share
Of blame, whose genius thus did somewhat dare.
Avaunt, too, social pleasantry, that seems
To clothe with ridicule all noble themes.
Said Fontenelle " This is my eightieth year;
And though a Frenchman, to whom jests are dear,
I never, throughout life, have sought to raise
A smile at the least thing that men should praise."
Oh, honour to the memory of those
Who could admire, and would great thoughts suppose!
Men who that private censorship ne'er fear'd
When in the lives of great men it appear'd—
A censorship whose strength was admiration
Existing in each breast and in each nation;
As when from documents all turn their eyes,
Indignant, when they hear that in them lies

The proofs against Metellus, which were brought,
By him demanded, and by them unsought;
For in his life they read his innocence,
And so defied these letters' insolence;
Or when of Afric's Scipio the foes
Came rushing, not as you would now suppose,
Not, sooth, to do him scathe and injury,
But only that they might the nigher see
The man whom they with such great joy admired,
Whose hands once kiss'd, transported, they retired;
Or as when the grave Senate rose in mass,
And to his prison would with Cato pass.

Then potent is this gift unto our race
To nourish genius, or its foes disgrace.
In Action, Reason, Memory, and Thought
The attributes of soul can best be sought;
But if of Admiration all amerced,
These qualities themselves seem quite reversed,
As can be witness'd in lethargic sprites
Whom no spur instigates, no joy delights.
How could they act who laziness admire?
How reason whom all mental efforts tire?
How remember aught when all is view'd
As mere provision for more lassitude?
How think, in fine, when what is counted best
Is a dull, soulless, and material rest?
Let Admiration once but fire the mind,
And all the four developed you will find,

Involving, too, Attention, which is said
To constitute alone within each head
The difference between the seeing eyes
And those whose scaly film all sight denies,
Save that which poor dumb animals can claim,
Identical with man's but in its name.
Attention shows the wondrous end of things,
And so reveals the whole your Minstrel sings,
Connects the smile on earth with smiles above,
Affection here commenced with endless love,
All that we see and hear, with somewhat more,
And so unlocks the bright enclosure's door.
It only needs you should attention spend,
To see on earth that nothing here does end.
So Admiration, which these views impart,
Transports with visions bright the human heart.
This gift I own, when fullest, silence brings,
Not many words, as Homer deeply sings.
So when Ulysses had his labours told,
His auditors " consulting " we behold,
With no vociferation, or yet praise,
But just as if astonish'd each one stays;
Which partly can explain why some are loud,
Extolling vain things that attract the crowd.
The earth, meanwhile, has sights so fair and grand,
That silent admiration they command;
And common mortals of untarnish'd mould
Cannot express, they own, what they behold.
They feel o'erwhelm'd by what they daily see,
By apparitions of such majesty.

Few are the words Apollo dictates then,
Forbidding much discourse with frantic men,
Who in their Forums cheer the loudest voice
Which is accordant winh their own vain choice.

But here a song didactic will require
A change of tone less simple on the lyre.

Wise critics say a book might be composed
    Of Rhetoric, entitled " The effects
Of Audience," where might clearly be disclosed
    Why one admires, and anon rejects
As worthless, the same poem, lecture, speech,
A fact of all experience within reach.

Take any writing, be it verse or prose,
    And read it then successively before
One who to disparage only knows,
    And one who can admire still more and more.
The Poet or the Orator will find
The page is wholly changed in his own mind;

That what, discouraged, he thought poor and vain,
    Becomes, the other hearing it, most grand;
The former audience had untuned the strain;
    The latter made it musical and bland.

The cause of all this wondrous transformation
Was in the gift or want of admiration [1].
"Effect of Audience" thus all genius rules,
Which can be wither'd by the breath of fools.
"No one," says Montesquieu, " would ever believe
To what excess this want has grown of late;
How greatly it does now our age deceive,
When deeming nothing beautiful or great;
For be it nature's charms or works of art,
For neither has this century a heart."
Now if you would the causes fully know,
La Harpe undraws a curtain, and will show.
For, lo! what strange conspirators are here!
'Tis Admiration that they hate and fear.
Long had the world enjoy'd its dulcet sway,
When first arose the Sophists of our day;
For though resisted by the public sound,
In England, as in France, they still abound;
Esteeming Admiration as a yoke
Imposed on others whom it should provoke.
The Regent and his court would thus laugh down
All those whose brows a glory true did crown—
A Boileau, Racine, Molière, or Rousseau,
The lyric, La Fontaine, or deft Quinault.
Each scene, epistle, or Pindaric ode
Was mark'd, condemn'd on their barbaric code.
And why? because they'd overthrow the sway
Of Admiration, which "had had its day."

[1] Ste. Beuve.

That gentle spirit was too close allied
To what opposed their diabolic pride.
It open'd wide Heav'n—views for them too vast—
And so they vow'd it should no longer last.
They'd have recourse to any paradox,
If but the way to Paradise it blocks.
Of Sophists even would they take the side
That Socrates's views might be denied:
But things incomprehensible appear,
By sly self-love interpreted, most clear;
As when it tells you Admiration must
Awaken feelings which they hate to trust.
Of goodness, faith, it then must share the fate,
And so be exiled from the Sophist's state.
The fiend that they would substitute for King
Must to his council scornful spirits bring;
And all his subjects whom he will inspire
Must never more what is on earth admire;
And so one straight way to Heav'n will be closed,
Abjured a yoke which Nature had imposed;
And men grown wild will shout, reprove, and scorn
And feel for mocking all things they were born—
Ay, even honour, as we see in France,
Where Europe's "brothers" their red flag advance—
Madden'd when aught of fair can meet their eye,
Mocking through life, with mockery to die.
"Oh, what a life, and what an age is here!"
Cries even Hugo, while he owns his fear.
" Power, and Goodness, Faith, and Genius too,
Whate'er the best will think, and say, and do;

All that remains of grandeur from the past
Is now condemn'd, as what no more must last;
Drawn on a hurdle, 'neath ignoble flags,
Hooted by Laughter and feign'd Mirth in rags."
Here is the focus, while the clouds that roll
So far and wide can grieve no less the soul.
Then wonder not if these should have success,
Yea, greater, wider than our words express.
So Boswell here becomes an endless jest
For having thought his hero wisest, best;
And friendship full of noble admiration,
Excites in us a kind of indignation.
Sevigné's burst of praise is thus a flower
Now seldom found within a rural bower.
The country mansion yields indeed its sport,
But not exactly pleasures of her sort;
Enthusiasm, like hers, for all things grand
Is what this skilful age cannot command.
Oh, who now in a public garden fair
Would hope to find, enchanted, seated there
Some high-born damsels who were thither drawn,
Assembled gaily on the cheerful lawn,
Chiefly to hear a man of genius speak,
Ulysses-like, and nought but tales to seek?
As when return' Maupertuis thus was found,
With these fond listeners all gather'd round.
Whatever genius may be thought to claim,
To use a common phrase, 'tis just the same.
Men now will mock Partenopax, of Blois,
Who when a simple white-wash'd wall he saw

Described it as of ivory a tower,
So sway'd was he by admiration's power.
The want of admiration now supplies
A weaker spirit that will criticize.
With cries of joy it counts its victim's moans,
As in a robber's cave men count on stones
The money they have gain'd by one good shot,
Kill whom it may, so they are poorer not.
Slaves to some richer slave, their captain then,
These writers watch all from their inky den,
Ambitious, climbing one upon the other,
Like ivy bent, whate'er they grasp to smother,
Which oft proves Worth, at least compared with
    those
Whose object is to kill what near them grows.
Worth, that at least disdains the vulgar way
On which all things are judged by what they pay;
Worth, that can pity clever men's long toil,
Who waste their talents for so mean a spoil.
But all are critics now who only grope,
Left without compass, star, or faith, or hope.
In nothing do we find aught to admire,
Till of ourselves, ourselves at last we tire.
In this one point at least we would agree
With what was held by ancient pedantry.
That Virgil's words were oft familiar, low,
Some gravest writers undertook to show;
Though later scholars proved how senseless, vain
Were their impressions when they did complain [1].

[1] Aul. Gel. lib. ii.

Some said that in a copy by his hand
The letter *h* was dropp'd, they understand [1].
Virgil a cockney; but you must expect
All from the present universal sect.
Who Lipsius and Scaliger recall,
Without their lore, their criticism all.
His geographic knowledge too they thought,
As well his chronologic, quite at fault.
Then others, too, would Sallust reprehend,
And show how they could oft his language mend.
But I would bid avaunt to all the crew,
Who joys of admiration never knew!
Mount to the Capitol let us, that so
Our manners may be those of Scipio,
And leave these triflers to their wonted ways,
While we pour forth with gratitude our praise.

CANTO VI.

BY ADMIRATION (WORKS OF ART, PAINTING, AND MUSIC).

Great Nature's works admired so, we said,
To fields Elysian men have often led.
But works of human art no less provide
A field for admiration truly wide;

[1] Aul. Gel. lib. ii. 3.

Whether they would exactly imitate
Sweet Nature's present and imperfect state;
Or striving to combine in one all parts
Of beauty, so as to inflame our hearts
By picturing an artificial whole,
Made up of parts, and no part copied sole.
While, on whatever pathway they would wend,
They all must seek this one essential end—
Of making the unseen to mind appear,
Without which nought that's seen is ever dear.
For so all works design'd of human art
That with success would touch and move the heart
Must still by means that are well known to all,
From things unseen remove the present pall,
That the invisible may clearly be
Brought thus before the mind; that ever we
May see its sheen, and feel its cheering glow;
For nought else moves the heart on earth below.
'Tis then that art will yield for mankind here
A foretaste of the bliss that will appear
In those fair, happy regions, where it may
Be not intended all to pass away.

The bliss of those who Nature will admire,
Descends no less on those who never tire
Observing Nature in men's works of art,
Of which a view they equally impart;
So that we argue justly when we hold
That human works can Heav'n itself unfold.

In song, the thought and sentiment come first;
   These reign and govern, and still will keep the heights;
In painting, howe'er purely artists thirst.
   The workman's hand will chiefly claim its rights—
Yes, even when it seeks the pure ideal,
And shuns an imitation of the real.

But if with skill you weigh the mystic bond,
   Connecting hands with the presiding soul,
Your thoughts disparaging will then prove fond,
   If raising not more wonder at the whole;
Or else, unless the hand rebels, and then
You well may scorn Art's democratic men,

Who seek but profit with much daily toil,
   By eccentricity, or what is worse,
By agency the human mind to soil
   And yield a bitter, and a cleaving curse.
Whereas it is Art's office to supply
A path towards Eden to attract the eye,

Supporting and exalting human life,
   As even Plato show'd in days of old,
Suggesting that its noble, endless strife
   Should be in making age and youth behold
The inner nature of the good and fair,
To fan their temples with Elysian air.

Though painting's aim is never to deceive,
   Like that which comes to aid dramatic art,
Impressions from its power you receive,
   As if the real truth had moved your heart.
You know 'tis all deception from the first,
'Tis from your mind alone its beauties burst.

So noble was this great pictorial art
   Esteem'd of old by the deep Grecian mind,
That slaves, it said, should never take a part
   In what to highest regions man could bind.
Their interdiction flow'd from evils past,
But it proved lofty views which still should last.

When Thaze's Polygnotus had devised
   With Micon the Athenian that great change
In painting which all artists so surprised
   By using ochre, and e'en, still more strange,
Four colours; since before their time, one tone
Belonged to all the painting that was known.

'Twas said perfection Art at once did gain;
   And such was then men's wondrous admiration
That warriors themselves would e'en refrain
   From conquests thought required by their nation,
Rather than paintings should endanger'd be
By their own long'd-for, glorious victory.

Demetrius thus raised the seige of Rhodes
    For the sole reason that he fear'd lest fire
Caused by his engines and war's other modes
    Might hurt the picture men did so admire.
By that one work Protogenes did save
The city doom'd to perish with the brave.

And then how grand and simple was the style
    Of praise elicited by noble art!
No words epigrammatic to beguile;
    The picture speaks sufficient to the heart.
So witness what Simonides did write,
That two clear lines may teach you what is right.

" Of Thaze Polygnotus, who was son
    Of Aglaophon, has this picture made "—
Only this written he deem'd all was done
    As if more words the artist would degrade;
He writes his name, that of his Father, down,
Then to give honours due, his native town.

Two thousand years ago men knew to praise
    The works of human art that should endure.
Then we, to whom they open brighter ways,
    Should nourish admiration still more pure,
When, led by them, we take the blissful road
Where Beauty reigns as in its first abode.

Saith Ruskin, "Making pictures bright is much,
   But giving brightness to our life is more"—
Ah! that proclaims the real Artist's touch,
   The Christian Artist as in days of yore.
Then art can ev'ry English homestead turn
Into a picture which will make hearts burn,

E'en as if painted by Bellini's hand,
   Or Cima's, glorious with the light of love,
As if on earth the work of God did stand
   All undegraded as in realms above,
As if with men here living, He did dwell,
And find in Earth's sweet garden all was well.

What men call works of Art are works Divine,
   So far as is the power they imply;
In them will only still more clearly shine
   (If that could e'er be said) of the Most High
The skill and power that could so endow
A creature who creates like Artists now.

The argument is trite, but what could be
   More wondrously surpassing nature's store,
Than if a watch contrived you were to see
   To make another and a thousand more?
In man who so creates a wonder lies
Which shows us best the Artist of the skies.

This Art is still a region of the earth;
    Though all the shapes of workmanship Divine
Have there a borrow'd dwelling, and their birth,
    Which to the mental eye prove genuine,
When imitative skill will there select
That with which God the Universe has deck'd.

Such Artists pass through Eden's happy plains;
    Their colours too, dipp'd in Heav'n, thence are
        drawn;
Divine effulgence their bright mind retains;
    Crystalline spheres announce to them the dawn;
Immortal Amaranth is round them spread;
Ambrosial fruitage bears the ground they tread.

For from the everlasting pleasure flows
    Each noble thought that comes into the mind;
To copy only each true Artist knows;
    Originals alone in God to find;
It is e'en through Heav'n therefore he must stray;
For find them elsewhere, sooth, he never may.

The beauty which he sees in tree and flower,
    The light that sheds soft lustre from the eye,
The glory seen when Fancy bright will tower—
    These will proclaim he is to Eden nigh;
While disunited with it all is clay,
Soulless and senseless, soon to pass away.

Saint Bonaventure says that Art can thus
    Disclose Eternal Beauty to the mind,
Throw open wide the portals unto us,
    When the celestial Paradise we find.
Theophilus expressly says that so
From God's own Spirit it must ever flow.

Then, mark, by what Art yields unto the sight,
    All those who see it can companions be,
In straying while on earth through Heav'nly light,
    As if they had forestall'd Eternity.
For e'en its lowest visions still are drawn
From what is seen through a celestial dawn.

Take landscapes, flowers, which it so commands,
    What doth proclaim the sky, the varied ground?
God's glory, and the work of His own hands,
    To realize the great Davidic sound;
And oft such painters, wise Murillo said,
Like Iriarte, had to Eden led.

Then Art can virtue teach, and so revive
    Another golden age within each breast;
For noble deeds of old will thus survive,
    And in their spirits great hearts find their rest,
As if in Eden's bowers, when they see
The human innocence and dignity.

The "manners-making" Art[1] then loves the poor.
  Callistratus, who call'd Art so, knew ill
The manners which it helps to make endure,
  When taught by it men charity fulfil.
But, led by that soft dame, the fragrant way
Through heav'nly fields and blissful woodlands lay.

Then oft through holy temples and the quire
  Art waves us to the saintly life of men.
And what displays it in these precincts higher?
  Heav'n's great glory wide thrown open then,
While the chief doctrines of our faith we see
Stamp'd on Truth's brightest scrolls eternally.

'Tis there mute Theologians find their crown;
  Sacro-pictorial codes have been their guide;
Before mysterious light they had cast down
  The bars which oft from Heav'n can souls divide;
Yea, visions, pray'd for, sometimes did impart
Celestial models to direct their Art.

When death, all stripp'd of terrors, they display,
  As in Saint Isidore, Saint Francis, Clare,
Saint Dominic—oh, whither did they stray,
  But through that Eden where was nought to scare,

---

[1] ἠθοποιῶν τέχνη.

No sorrow enter'd, and no death was made
To blight the blossoms of its happy shade?

And so, in fact, we know their steps were led;
   For holy lives they spent while treading earth;
To Christ their fervent spirits ever wed,
   They knew while here what fills the heavens with mirth;
Would I could now the names of some recall!
But Faith, and Hope, and Love, belong'd to all.

Ah! you may rake up seeds from richest mould,
   Importing flow'rets not from Eden's soil;
Repeat you may what is of Raphael told,
   And make of all his faults a hideous coil;
But there will lie, still cover'd, the pure spring
In which his soul did dip her heav'nly wing.

What skills it to advance exceptions now,
   Where Art has fallen from its glorious height;
And those who best observe it will allow
   That its chief adepts see no Heav'nly light.
Sooth, not through Eden have they pass'd to tell
The sole experience that they think is well.

Alas! through other fields they must have stray'd,
   When each seems anxious hideous things to tell
And what he hears conversant with the shade
   Where vilest spirits wander on through Hell.

But to these few who mock the just and right,
We only say, "Avaunt! and quit our sight."

Let art unfold and sound her wondrous power,
    Let Painting, Music, Sculpture, all be here—
We find ourselves in an unearthly bower,
    Where all is sweet and noble, soft and dear;
Our human admiration brings us nigh
To Heav'n and its great joys, supreme and high.

I will not works of ancient times recall;
    Let present Art alone be heard and seen,
Rossini, Herbert, Calderon, I call,
    With Millais, and still countless more between.
What do we mark in those who feel this spell?
A starting tear, proclaiming all is well.

Observe those "Orphans" singing in the snow;
    Behold that babe who in its cradle floats,
That boy who listens, seeking more to know,
    Raleigh, who, young, upon the ocean dotes.
What think you, then, of painters in our day?
Of their divine and universal sway?

Or, lo! within the grim Tower you can stand
    Beholding More, so tranquil and serene—
What grandeur Herbert's pencil can command
    When that sublime and tearful group is seen!
No effort to display dramatic art;
'Tis passionless resolve that awes your heart.

Or let the organs sound, the "Stabat" rise,
  The grand "Laudate" which made turn aghast
The Priest who offer'd the great sacrifice—
  Man's exile and a disjoin'd world are pass'd;
Then Heav'n and earth are one—no need of prayer,
'Tis love, 'tis Heav'n's own raptures that are there.

Nor is this admiration ever vain:
  The Saints are never weary praising song;
And instruments to aid the dulcet strain,
  To sacred science, both, say they, belong.
Cassiodorus and Augustin sage
Have eulogized them on their lofty page.

Our Roger Bacon, as with Music fired,
  Maintains that song all evil can dispel;
With love for the invisible inspired,
  He says that man, by Music, learns to quell
All bad excess of passions which can bind
To things of body his most noble mind.

He treats on the utility of sound
  Thus musical, with dancing of the feet,
With postures, gestures, pleasing all around,
  Harmonious as the strain itself is sweet;
Which works are mathematical, he shows,
From Science sprung, and truths that mankind knows.

" Such admiration is," saith he, "innate,"
  Common to all the world; and from the first
Of sciences it flows, past all debate,
  By means of which all men can quench their thirst;

Which science youths and rudest rustics own,
And without which no other can be known.

Then easy is the way by Music, so
    By movements ever in proportion, thus
To reach Elysium, whither all would go,
    And find the entrance open unto us,
By hearing and by sight its golden doors
Unfolded, while this twofold sense adores[1].

The charm of Music lies not in its sound,
    As if in its reception by the ear;
But deep within the human heart 'tis found
    Reveal'd when thus its melodies we hear.
Thence, not from strings or wind it draws those tones
Which the moved soul so acted upon owns.

There is the wondrous magic of its power,
    When, instantly descending thus below,
It draws from hearts, as from a mystic bower,
    What causes thought, and joy, or tears to flow,
What would without it ever dormant lie
In these strange depths of our humanity.

But what is drawn thus, whether grave or gay,
    Belongs unto the wings with which we soar,
Comes not from earth, though in our hearts it lay,
    But tells of what we lost in days of yore,
Of what we may more fully here regain,
Whether to dance or mourn should prompt the strain

[1] Op. tert. c. 53.

Yea, tells it too of what we have regain'd,
   The moment that we catch the potent sound;
For joy, however short, is there maintain'd—
   Such bliss as re-unites this mortal ground
With that mysterious and transcendant whole
For which we feel was made and tuned the soul.

Superfluous does Music seem to be;
   All other gifts on earth will serve mankind;
Yet this, of noble inutility,
   Can the most deeply move the human mind.
For here, the more it seems without an end,
The more to boundless good it seems to tend.

Hail! sweet Musician, haste and play,
   And make thy instrument respond
To the deep raptures that will sway
   Thy mind so lofty, and so fond.
     Silent be Earth! attend!
     'Tis through Eden he will wend.
     From the moment he begins
     This very silence entrance wins.
     Lifted be fingers to each lip
     Ambrosia about to sip.
     A rapt expectant thus to be
     To Elia was felicity.
     O Silence, how divine thou art!
     Thou thyself canst bliss impart.
     Silentium is thus the first
     Defile through which will Eden burst.

See you not how all remain
Expecting? soon will fall the strain
Upon the ravish'd heart of those
In whom true admiration glows,
Who may exemplify again
What Plutarch says of such a strain,
That it can wind up or let down,
Like laws that change a state or town,
As Solon and Lycurgus play'd,
And, as it were, by Music made
The alterations we admire
Compared to those caused by the Lyre.

But, hark! he sweeps the notes that flow,
His transports to prepare, foreshow;
And aye a prelude comes before
When days are bright or tempests roar.
It is a wild and rambling sound;
The passage has not yet been found—
Lightly hither, lightly there,
A flying circuit every where.
Those who will participate
In all his raptures, though so great,
Seem now to be waiting, and half lost in doubt,
As if they would all his deep meaning find out;
Till by degrees, in quicker time,
      The tone that floats
      Hearts' joy denotes
In a playful, sparkling chime.

CANTO VI.

> Hark! how the quick sound
> Enamels the ground—
> 'Tis sweet summer's light,
> 'Tis Eden all bright,
> 'Tis frolic, not rest,
> As feet will attest;
> To dance each would rise,
> 'Tis joy of the skies.

Then when simple airs must change,
Science still through them will range.
Nimble hands with fingers light
Make to caper in your sight
The notes which now must skip and dance,
Retire, wheel round, anon advance,
His arms negligently thrown
From side to side, as if the tone
He still most rashly improvised,
Content if you were but surprised;
> Frolicking here,
> Frolicking there,

Nothing for gladness with him can compare.
> Words short,
> All sport,
>   Slow,
>   Low,
>   Proud,
>   Loud,
>   Wild,
>   Mild,

Then passionate, hasty, and retorting with fire,
They impel you to hate, or to love, or admire,
While, as questioning, answering, pleading, judging
 for all,
The changes, rapidly passing, quite bewilder, appal.
  One time distinct to every ear,
  Another blended, nothing clear,
  The sounds will skim or soar on high,
  Alike to them the ground or sky.
   Now quaint,
   Then faint,
Until the strain, past e'en almost beyond
All limits known to earth, so sweet and fond,
Protracted, lengthening ever as it flies,
As if dissolved in its own sweetness, dies.
Then, lo! with both arms placed across their
 breast,
And head thrown back as to attest
How deeply from their very soul they feel
What Music by its changes can reveal,
I mark the auditors, who seem
Rapt in a soft, delicious dream;
For now most grave the harmony will flow,
With tones impressive, scarcely moving, slow,
Till, fading into sentiment, the tear
Can tell what real tragedies appear;
For even in Heaven memory must be,
To waken and maintain true sympathy.
Then soft and gently flows the plaintive sound,
Sweet as e'er breathed the air o'er Eden's ground,

By the hills that rise above,
By the slopes as made for love,
By the winding stream that glides,
By the vale with blooming sides;
While waving hands of auditors betray
How hearts when soften'd dote upon the way.
For hands of auditors become the slaves
Of the musician when he loves or raves.
The streaming sweetness through the floodgate rolls,
And hurries with it bathed and raptured souls—
Falling and rising with the strain above,
Till all seems cover'd with one tide of love.
  The lengthen'd tones still fall and rise;
  Each to surpass in sweetness tries,
  As if 'twere more than man can bear,
  So passing through the liquid air,
Accentuated sharp, with bursts of sound,
Which seem to leave no force in all around,
As though, in fine, they ne'er could find an end,
Save in the bounds to which all wishes tend.
The strain with fitful gleams at last expires,
Lost in the glow of its consuming fires.
Then Heaven and Earth as to fond arms are won,
The dead and living kiss'd, as if in one.

  But, hark! each note now loud,
  Awakes the dozing crowd;
  With force each tone prolong'd,
  Asks aid for all the wrong'd;

'Tis wrath and fire
Each moment higher;
The harsh debate
Seems breathing hate,
No discord, yet opposing sounds
Almost attaining discord's bounds;
Yes, opposition, stern and fierce,
That would its adversaries pierce,
Augments the magic of the potent spell
And shouts the secrets which they would not tell.
As when a crowd beholds artistic fires,
The fulgurations which it so admires,
And still faster and faster the sparkles will fly,
They fall rushing round you, then mount to the sky
And motionless remain in upper air,
Grand planetary lights, divinely fair,
Till a loud shriek prolong'd, as a star sent alone,
Darting up to the zenith, where it bursts, and is gone,
Leaves but blank wonder and silence around
Through the shades of the night o'er the wide, darken'd ground,—
So here is a pause, amazement, and a cry,
Announcement of some happy victory;
Till by degrees the whole will fade away,
Reduced once more to Nature's tranquil sway;
And then with solemn majesty the strain
Grows calm, with mighty grandeur slow again.
It is as if all now saw, satisfied,
The host of martyrs who for justice died.

But Joy will raise her head, and soon invade
The pensive glory of the blissful shade ;
And fresh sounds all capricious will frolic and play ;
   And then all seem
   As if lost in a dream,
To dance like sprites, mirthful upon the flowing way.
Then, hark! an ascending scale alternately
Again soon descending, soft and pleasantly,
  With semitones in series long,
  Will sound the scientific song.
  For vague is now the mystic flow
  Of Heav'n's high language here below.
   The mind lost in thought
   Finds thus what it sought—
   Half wishes now whole,
   Contented in soul.
   Yes ; the great and the less,
   Which it dared not express,
   All bathed in delight,
   With Eden in sight,
Mistrust and fears for ever wholly fled,
The soul to truth and goodness ever wed.
  But dangers still beset the way,
  When over earth to Heaven we stray.
  In mingled fray, then, art with art
  Contends to claim the wavering heart.
Dintinctly all brought out, transparent, clear,
Italian sharp horizons as if near,

'Tis individuality that reigns;
'Tis Passion uncontroll'd that now complains.
The rapt musician seems to eye the deep
Where waves, like passions, will no longer sleep.
There is a hoarse demand, an awful pause;
With arms extended, a long dash he draws;
There is an awe-struck moment full of doubt;
There is defiance, and a wrathful shout.
The diabolic advocate begins,
As if the secret question were, Who wins?
  Now the great magician see,
  How he finds rapidity,
  As if with himself he wrangles,
  In his strain himself entangles;
  It is a flight, and each will try
  Who will gain the victory;
  Swift assertions and replies
  Each to chase the other flies;
  Quick suggestions, wild and rash,
  Are answer'd by a sudden thunder crash;
  And then, as if to rouse up all,
  Loud, sharp is heard the trumpet's call;
  When volleys of deep murmuring sound
  Make tremble all the distant ground;
  And the dense rising mountain cloud
  Each note will mingle and enshroud
  In undistinguishable mass,
  Till, rolling o'er the darken'd pass,
  Thick volumes end the fearful fray;
  And then once more shines out the day.

CANTO VI.

   Hark! hark! the foe is slain;
   'Tis Innocence again!
When, glorious conqueror, he breathes new life,
And sings his triumph in the noble strife,
Enthroned, victorious, risen there on high
In music's heaven through an ecstasy,
In the Empyræum bright of sound,
With Paradise regain'd, for ever found.
Then melodious torrents pass along
Of sound which give the victory to song,
To what is most divine within the soul,
Crown'd, all the lower passions to control,
Which, like the multitude, should still obey
Of truth and goodness the majestic sway;
For this means only that they thereby find
The peace of joy of Heaven in the mind.
   So victorious and strong
   O'er all that is wrong,
The hands seem multiplied as they
Are over the loud-sounding notes stretch'd to play;
   Aghast the rest stand,
   And obey the command,
With joy all triumphant to pass on the way;
   Though now 'tis ecstasy
   That they hear and they see;
   As the sounds louder rise,
   The forms surprise;
   They float in the air,
   All scatter'd their hair;

　　　　They need not the ground;
　　　　Nought earthly is found;
　　　　No arm is at rest;
　　　　Each will rapture attest.
The very notes aloft seem whirl'd on high,
As if the loud confusion reach'd the eye.
The grand Finale crashing on its way,
Subdues the hearers with its all-potent sway.
As wheels revolving rapidly are seen,
One circle and nought filling it between.
Or as when circling fast one note will fly
Multiplied, and no present sharpest eye
Can see there is in fact but only one
Whirl'd swiftly round, scarce view'd when it is
　　　gone—
So the musician skilful that you see
Draws countless notes with such rapidity,
That you would think in sight, not two, but ten
Hands spread out wide were dash'd all playing then.
Cheerfully, playfully, angrily, merrily, earnestly,
　　　changefully, all
Sound as if skilfullest, happiest, mightiest, homeliest,
　　　stateliest call.
Then louder slower tones together press,
Till breaks the wild storm which they can't com-
　　　press.
One tempest of indistinguishable sound
Sweeps o'er the terrified and darken'd ground,
　　　Levels mountains with thunder,
　　　Which bursts all asunder

CANTO VI.

      The bands that confined
      The vast strength of the mind.
See how to earth they no longer are bound!
How Heav'n's bright entrance on earth has been
    found!
Long had supremely elegiac strains
Well represented Nature that complains;
The voice of all the common social wants
Which patient meditation pensive haunts,
As when the German thought will slowly flow
And cause oblivion of the earth below—
Of memories, desires, and hopes, and fear,
The truest representative appear,
As moving veil'd, mysterious as a dream,
Till suddenly, distinct each form will gleam,
So will the notes, diffused like echoes long,
The world invisible invoke by song;
But now 'tis more than thoughtful contempla-
    tion;
It is a harmony as of creation;
The rapt musician seems to catch a tone
Ne'er audible except in Heav'n alone.
      The hum'rous strings are soft and sweet;
      Their thrill no echo dares repeat,
      Each striving to be heard in vain,
      While chaos seems the swelling strain;
      Though practised ears distinguish all
      As they flutter, mount, and fall,
      The harmony still varied, such
      Created by his learnëd touch;

While others hear a mingled din,
Announcing that he is within
The centre of that perfect gladness
Which to mortal ears seems madness,
All vast varieties in one
Loud diapason, Heaven won.

And the hearers, bent low with reverential joy,
  Bravissimo cry out,
  With an applausive shout,
As if lost in rapture, gestures strange employ.
 While he with folded arms stands
 As one who all the world commands,
 Contented, and supremely blest,
 Enjoying honour, and at rest.
Nor need the sweet enthusiast recoil
From these just praises, his own precious spoil—
 If love of praise were always wrong,
 It would not to our race belong;
But there is a glory which ever will roam,
  And from Heav'n it descends,
  Thither all desire bends,
Until it guides us gently to our true and lasting
  home.
 Let Music admiration rightly win,
 And Heaven is without us and within.
Nor deem unsuited to these blissful ways
The sweet contentment of well-earn'd praise,
That ever-bubbling spring so freshly yields
The stream that guides us to th' Elysian fields,

When dallying sweetness plays with what is hard,
And never will humility discard,
Plays ever lowly in that downy nest,
Where breed the thoughts and virtues that are best.
'Tis those who hate all praise that farthest fly
From the sweet plants that yield humility.
The bashful, all-confiding love of praise
With panting efforts still through heaven strays.
She labours long with hope in that sweet soil,
But never so as hearts or minds to spoil.
The groundwork of her song is hope and love,
And all her joy but leads her still above
The selfish passions of a mind diseased,
Which with itself alone is ever pleased.
Praise is for her the tribute only due
To Him who gave her all she ever knew;
And richly she repays those echoes wild,
Which leave her as they found her—still a child.
She gives them back the joys of admiration,
The fruits of her own power of creation
Entrusted to her, given, not her own
In Sculpture, Painting, and in Music's tone,
Not the less humble, not less good and true,
When feeling she herself does something too.
Her little soul so ravish'd with delight,
And conscious ever that her thoughts are right,
Receives the homage of th' admiring crowd,
As one whom deep humility does shroud;
Poor simple instrument, just like her own,
And feeling that nought else she e'er is grown,

But only fitted to obey the nod
Of her own nature tuned and touch'd by God.

But woe, alas! how many still are found
    Insensible and mute as stocks and stones,
Adhering without mind unto the ground,
    Blind to all grandeur, deaf to thrilling tones!
Such are most critics now, and even worse
The languid victims of soft Comfort's curse.

What did Beethoven in skill'd judges find?
    What did the tender and inspired Mozart?
Accusers, scorners, auditors unkind,
    Who wrote as men without an ear or heart.
Yet deeper sinks the poison that will stay
When Languor sums up all she has to say.

Euripides and Zeuxis might disdain
    Their critics, and all judgments but their own;
And Antigenidas might bid the strain
    Sound for the Muses, and for him alone;
But words like these cannot be now allow'd;
And all must slumber with the passive crowd.

Professional disparagers are now
    All but those few who urge a fond complaint;
Where lies the last appeal? you must allow,
    With slaves of luxury, grown feeble, faint,
Who would not lift their satiated eyes
To view the beauty of Ausonian skies.

What skills it to display the works of art
  When men are to all Nature's beauty blind?
Soft, pamper'd ease has robb'd them of their heart;
  In them nor eyes nor ears can any find.
For them all admiration is a word
Senseless, mistaken, and, in brief, absurd.

From Venice to Bologna let them stray,
  Let the Euganian hills stand rosy bright,
Through purple mountains let them take their way,
  Let rivers, vineyards, temples be in sight;
They see the cushion where they sit at ease;
But nothing else lethargic eyes will please.

Perhaps they'll faintly wish to speak of each;
  And then a comic feature changes all,
As when some feudal castle they will reach
  And from their lips astounding words will fall,
Like hers who said, "La Bretesche can much please:
'Tis quaint, 'tis fine, 'tis Gothic, 'tis Chinese!"

Not so when works of nature in man's art
  Are seen by fervent Love and Faith and Mind;
'Tis then that skill can play the noble part,
  For which it was imparted to our kind,
To kindle admiration's holy fire,
And pity, goodness, and great deeds inspire,

With love for beauty, which commences here,
  Which draws down Heav'n to our own earthly
    bow'rs,
In greater sheen at last to disappear,
  When Time itself will end with mortal hours,

L

While even here anticipated; though
The bounds of each we cannot clearly know.

But what is this that lifts us to the sky?
  'Tis not what's deem'd the prize that art should
    win,
The dealer's jargon, or the practised eye
  That lets, or lets not pictures enter in.
'Tis least of all, as I am very sure,
The admiration of a connoisseur,

Or judgments of committees, which, in fine,
  Are of dissembled hates th' association,
Of vanities combined a fruitful mine,
  Of spites all subtilized a concentration,
A wretch collective, ne'er to give account
For all its crimes whate'er be the amount.

But let the files of youths and women flow,
  Of children doting on their nurse or guide,
Intelligent and curious, as you know,
  Half awe-struck, clinging to some aged side;
While hearing, or else pointing out with glee
Some wondrous scene that moves their phantasy.

Then let the canvas speak; and what you see
  In those who hear its grand or tender voice
The truest confirmation aye will be,
  Which leaves you thenceforth now no other
    choice,

But simply to confess it ever yields
An entrance to the true Elysian Fields.

If (to recur to Virgil's lofty song)
 Æneas in Sidonian Dido's fane
We see attracted, gazing, thoughtful, long,
 His mind still feeding on its pictures vain,
Standing and weeping as he studied each,
While marking how they great events could teach,

Naming each figure as it grandly stood,
 Saluting each with deep and tearful moans;
When for the first time then he understood
 The land he came to, human feeling owns,
What cannot painting work in later times,
Whose voice re-echoes the eternal chimes?

When holy subjects thus should meet the eyes,
 Some scene of Christ's great goodness to recall,
The rich, I heard once said, would criticize;
 But down upon their knees the poor would fall;
And genius that admires aught thus is ever
Poor, just like these, and like such fulness never.

How often portraits can transport us back
 To noble times when truth was magnified,
From which we now turn with sinistrous track,
 As if success had crown'd the strife of pride;
But faces such have always much to tell
Of Heav'n's own secrets which on them can dwell

Ask who these men were once, and hear them speak;
  For they have much to say of that bright clime
Through which they pass'd on earth, and ever seek
  To follow where they led in ancient time,
Or ask why fair, loved creatures pass'd away,
Then, blind to all views of Heaven, cease to stray.

If portraits thus should represent the dead,
  The bosom heaves, the eye expanded grown,
Is seen bedew'd with tears, while nought is said;
  But there is witness'd, tender hearts will own,
The Blessed Fields, for us, the silent Land,
Where safe for ever live the good and grand.

Yes, portraiture, like learning, can unfold
  A thread to guide our hearts through Eden's flowers—
The souls of men whose honours have been told
  By angels, in the sweet celestial bowers,
Where only such desire to be known,
And others fear not that they should be shown.

Saith Ruskin, " 'Tis the highest aim of Art,
  To set before you one thus truly grand,"
That, seeing, you may read within his heart
  How nought that's base on earth could him command,
Nought there deceptive, or what only seems,
But the true greatness, as in glorious dreams.

How oft to me this lesson is convey'd
  In presence of some maid who silent stands
Before the picture, while the others stray'd,
  As if nought there attention deep commands,
While she, too full to speak, remains alone,
Rapt by heart's eloquence, and that her own.

Perhaps she sees the early faithful friend
  Who said to her, "You only please my heart,"
Who chose her therefore, and for that sole end,
  As if his wisdom Ovid did impart;
For nature thus will never lead astray
Those who will follow her impulsive way.

She sees the front that never vaunted lore,
  From pedantry, and all its airs so far;
The love more vocal than its learnëd store,
  Of which the jargon can love's sweetness mar;
She hears the words so popular and bland
Which made familiar to her soul the grand.

Yes, what hears she? whom does she then be-
      hold?
  Her hero's voice, the loved one of her heart.
'Tis vital presence—'tis corporeal mould,
  From her in Heav'n's bright fields no more to
      part.
So admiration thus, by human skill, supplies
A union here with joy beyond the skies.

Such admiration has a magic way
Of causing moments like whole years to stay,
Impressing on the mind in passing time
What seems to antidate th' Eternal chime,
For one short instant causing us to see
As if the sum of all felicity.
  Before a crucifix, alone,
  And motionless, as turn'd to stone,
  Murillo, it is said, was found,
  Insensible to all around,
  Absorb'd, so wholly lost in thought,
  That nothing his attention caught.
  The Sacristan would then complain
  That he should there so long remain,
  Almost as if he even slept;
  So urging him to move he kept.
  " For what now stay you?" then he said;
  " Why are you waiting? Hence be sped."
  " I'm waiting so," he then replied,
  " To see them take that wounded side
  Down from the cross, where I behold
  More wonders than the earth has told,
  Or ever will while time does last,
  So deeply I admire the past."
  What think you of that admiration?
  Of that rapt, quiet contemplation?
  Its fruits at once you clearly see
  Are Heaven reveal'd mysteriously.
  Alas! I fear it is not thus
  That admiration comes to us,

Who cast a hasty look, and on
Stray, all impatient to be gone.
And yet this year a youth who lay
A dying had still this to say :—
" Oh, take me to the church once more,
And place me then beside the door
Where yet I can my Saviour see
As dead, and dead like that for me."
His words were these—" Once more I'd pop
Into the church, and there I'd stop."
So admiration still can sway
The humble young folk of our day.
Yet who would think such things could be
As blaming sensibility,
And blaming Art for occupying
Men's minds about our Saviour dying—
As styling it a morbid gloom
Which must for action leave no room?
And blaming Christian women's view,
When they His sepulchre renew ;
As if it were not thoughts like these
That yield the wonders that one sees
In deeds of tender charity,
Though springing all spontaneously,
And as if those who knew them not,
To comfort others ne'er forgot!

Yet 'tis high genius and a noble heart
That thus complain to make men's conscience start,

And breathe with fervency a silent prayer,
That faith may visit him who thus can scare.
  In mediæval times, at least,
  Religious painting was a feast
  For those who held that by such art
  Men must in Heav'n have had their heart;
  "And artists in this way devout,"
  Says Heisterbach, "will, past a doubt,
  Have special recompense above
  If they have always work'd for love
  Much rather than for earthly gain,
  Which would have made their labour vain.
  A monk of a great order black,
  Near Mayence, but a short time back,
  Who thus had painted in his time
  Unnumber'd pictures and sublime,
  Showing Christ's Passion, had for prize
  That on Good Friday he too dies.
  Deliver'd on the self-same day,
  Rewarded thus, he pass'd away[1]."
  But there are stranger things to tell
  Of Admiration's potent spell.
  Another instance from our store
  Now take which can astonish more.
  A monk, 'tis said, who matins sung
  His hooded brothers all among,
  When coming to the words that say,
  "A thousand years are but a day,

---

[1] Lib. viii.

For those who see the throne Divine,
Whence glories on the angels shine,"
Began to think how that could be,
And fell into a reverie
When all the rest had left the quire,
Where he remain'd but to admire,
And pray that God the mode would show
That he the meaning whole might know.
Scarce ended was his secret prayer,
When, lo! a little bird was there,
From arch to arch still flying, singing,
And to his pensive heart joy bringing,
Until at length, and by degrees,
She lures him to the greenwood trees
Which sprinkled shadows all around
That meditative verdant ground.
Perch'd on a branch she sung her song
Nor did the interval seem long
To him who listen'd with delight,
And, like to some poetic wight,
Lapp'd in Elysium, so to say,
Which words denote where ends that way.
  At length the birdie left its stalk;
  The monk did back to convent walk,
  The while quite pensive, if not sad,
  Thinking on joys that might be had.
  It seem'd to him the hour of Tierce,
  As through the greenwood he did pierce;
  Knowing he had left the quire when
  Matins had sung the hooded men;

But coming to the convent door,
O wonder! it was there no more.
He search'd, and found another gate,
And there commenced a strange debate
Between him and a porter new,
One whom before he never knew.
His name was ask'd, and business there,
He told it—saw the other stare,
Who bade him then the Abbot name,
The Prior, Sacristan, the same;
He named them; and then all the while
He saw th' interrogator smile,
Who would refuse him entrance, till
He signified to him his will
To be unto the Abbot shown,
That all might then be clearly known.
Presented to the Abbot, he
A total stranger then did see,
And who, moreover, knew him not,
As if all bonds were quite forgot.
The Abbot ask'd if he could tell
The abbot's name he knew so well,
Who, hearing it, himself applied
To annals ranged in cases wide,
Where soon he found the name inscribed,
And all the rest, who were described
As having lived long while ago—
Three hundred years since then did flow!
Received back as a brother there,
For Paradise he did prepare.

Thus Admiration then did yield
An entrance to the Heav'nly field.
Away might pass three hundred years
If but a ray from Heav'n appears;
The pleasure of one sense inspires
(When aught man cordially admires)
A rapture from which time will fly
To yield place to eternity;
For doubtless while the bird remain'd
Eternity was there maintain'd,
As far as joy meant, which ne'er knows
Abatement in itself or close.
The man may still draw mortal breath,
But bliss like that can fear no death—
Immortal in its source, whence flow
The rills that ravish men below.

CANTO VII.

TO YOUTH.

But here the simple strain must change,
 As now through human life we range,
To show how in his youth and age,
As in his intermediate stage,
Man, while still walking on the earth,
Can mingle in that heav'nly mirth
Which reigns where he unconsciously
Can fly in mind, as if to see

The place of gladness evermore.
So passing back through Eden's door.
Though wild, above all rule or art,
Enormous bliss within the heart,
Both youth and childhood have their gleams
Of light surpassing all our dreams,
Which, in their sweet and early hours,
Will yield bright tints to earthly bowers;
As rays material paint the rose,
And every beauteous thing that grows;
And these are what we often call
Affinities which open all
The paths and glades that never end
Until through Heav'n's own bliss they wend.
In ancient manuscripts I find
Youth painted as to charm the mind;
With wings expanded at his feet,
His looks and gestures are most sweet.
Yet painting has contrived to say
That still his heart is set on play;
For on his hand a ball is shown—
The rapture is to have it thrown.
But still those feet so plumed with wings
Tell facts as if a poet sings;
For though as Philopæmon tall,
Each lad a child you still might call;
Though him the Spartans would have class'd
'Midst "Irens," or, what them surpass'd,
"Mellirens," elder lads, so named,
A child he's still and not ashamed.

Youth's vulgar pleasures e'en can be
A source of true felicity ;
For folly 'twere to leave it nought
But gravity in act and thought.
To ride, to swim, to play and romp,
Far from the ways of worldly pomp,
To please all common eyes by things
Of which each knightly poet sings,
As when he tames his roadster fine
By means the shyest can divine,
To please, to help, to serve another,
Prove joys that time will never smother ;
And though the means you may deride,
What nature meant no sage can hide,
And that is simple, youthful joy,
That well becomes the valiant boy ;
To whom, as in Wordsworthian songs,
So much of earth and Heav'n belongs.
So while thus low at times it flies,
Anon to soar the heart will rise
Unclogg'd, for all you say, by earth,
To taste what in Heav'n had its birth.
Youth hails the true Aurora's rays ;
And skies more bright arrest its gaze ;
A something than the earth more fair
Shines all around it every where.
Sweet morning of the human mind,
When Eden on the earth we find !
As windows open to the day,
So youth will keep its joyous way

Of throwing open its whole mind
To all that's lovely, sweet, and kind.
And, what is strange, though strictly true,
With gladness Wisdom enters too;
While men are fretful, weary, sad,
Youth is, without their reasoning, glad.

I shall not always stop to tell
How each affinity suits well
The fount, the grove, the flow'ry plains,
Where bliss each circumstance maintains,
Or Alpine hills when distant towns
Will pour to wander on those downs
Their populous and joyful young,
To climb the rocks and ice among;
For higher than the virgin Peak
Is the great summit youth will seek.
Some salient traits suffice to show
Where lead its ways, that we may know
Mysteriously on youth will shine
The true, the good, and the Divine.
For, naturally pious, youth
Will love, not shun religious truth;
And so Paulinus shows at first
The fruits of its angelic thirst.
For, when grave seniors crucified
Our Lord, and Him old men denied,
The young a joyful triumph gave
To Him who came the world to save.

No bars stop ways that lead to joy,
When trusting, loving with each boy ;
While hoping, too, as ever will
All those who quaff youth's crystal rill.
No sophistry will taint the air ;
So minds inhale the good and fair ;
And where the heart is never proud,
No earthly darkness eyes will shroud.
Youth's curiosity is such,
That this alone assists it much.
Young London great attention pays
To every object it surveys ;
It likes to peep into a hole,
Each work of mankind to control ;
And oft, in fact, the well of truth
Is the best fathom'd by mere youth.
That Well itself reflects youth's face,
On which refracted rays we trace.
There is to us, as Virgil sings,
Much youth that hath seen many things,
Though no Æneas may be here
Proclaiming it to every ear ;
And then its nature, as we know,
Can visions manifold bestow.
For youth unconsciously obeys ;
And humble are its daily ways.
No boughs conceal the bubbling spring
Whence flows each bright translucid thing
Belonging to that sacred Pale
Where truth, not kings, must aye prevail.

Youth's air is vocal to proclaim
Truth's ever blest and glorious name.
The young, most sweetly without vaunt,
Will truth's high, solemn precincts haunt;
To them, when once with guidance sped,
Truth hastens with a nimble tread—
A fact to be remark'd by those
'Gainst whom old guides will Eden close,
As "Correspondents" of our press
Who seldom wear a youthful dress.
When sent to Rome they letters write
Which manifest their senile spite.
In their coarse, scornful language then
I see broad-bearded, whisker'd men—
The kind of figures that will frown
From club-house windows here in Town,
Or smile with that sinistrous air
Which puts to flight the good and fair.
The lad that whistles, sings, or cries,
Would gaze on her with other eyes;
With pen in locks behind his ear,
For truth a steady volunteer,
He'd see the halo round her head
(And what he sees is simply said)—
But youthful nature cannot see
What justifies vulgarity,
When working, like a clown well paid,
'Midst ruins he himself has made.
Affinities with Heav'n has youth,
Though rude, affinities with truth.

Saint Maur had but eleven years
When thus on Sion he appears.
Saint Placidus had counted seven
When he did give himself to Heaven.
At the same age did Faustus, Bede,
And Mechtild no less to Heav'n speed.
Marina d'Escobar at three—
Far more than all she loved to see—
Loved God. And what does that explain,
But that with her no joy proved vain?
Saint Hildegard was eight years old
When she did all this sheen behold.
Petrus Diaconus at five
Did thus at Heav'n's bright gate arrive;
As did Saint Boniface, who gain'd
The crown which no false glory stain'd.
Panormitanus, but a youth
Of thirteen summers, walked with Truth;
As at the age of sixteen years
Alcantara's bright saint appears.
I name but few—what could we tell
If private households we knew well?
Whose young, like these, on this earth trod,
Beholding Eden, hearing God?
Oh, my John Gerald, such wert thou!
In dreams alone I see thee now.
The star-like smiles of common youth
Can still proclaim this ancient truth.
While some in our age scorn the name
Of child or good, as yielding shame,

M

The wise old term can still apply
To many as we pass them by.
Yes, " good child," and at every age
Will each still be a gladsome sage!
" Too childish, foolish, for this world,"
As Gloucester says, while through it whirl'd,
Encompass'd with a mystic light
Which turns the sun to murky night,
Lured, as wing'd insects, through the air
By the near radiance shining there.
So Villanova's Thomas cries,
" What bliss with that of children vies?"
O golden age of maidens, boys,
Whose faces e'en proclaim their joys!
Behold them as they swing through air,
With all the Graces playing there.
To make them angels what is left
Of their pure gladness not bereft?
Yes, what is wanting? still he cries,
For though thus wingless each one flies.
For them are earth and Heav'n but one,
As if mortality were gone.
No house, perhaps, that does not hear
Some tones from Eden floating near
In childhood's words, as dropp'd by chance,
Which e'en hard bosoms can entrance,
That marks not traits of nature fine
Which for the moment seem Divine—
Some word, some question, some reply,
That shows how youth to God is nigh.

Ah, what sweet idyls then might sing
A poet, not those of the king,
But of the child, the boy, or maid,
Fresh from the true Elysian shade!
Oh, say what is thy children's bower
But Heav'n here in a finite hour?
For me to think of little John
On earth, then Heav'n with it is one.
Lætitia, Mary, Thomas, see,
What pure, what vast felicity!
Neither was tall Marcella found
A flower foreign to such ground;
Nor yet Kenelmus, ever grave,
And less inclined to romp and rave.
But all enjoy'd, and did impart
Of these bless'd fields not small a part.
Nor facts beheld would I confine
To those young plants that I call'd mine;
For such no doubt is every where
Th' effects of man's bright morning air,
At least, when shelter'd from the blight
That taints young hearts e'en to the sight.
Eden is seen where'er you stray
With them and watch their joyful way,
Yes, questionless, e'en in the street,
Enjoy'd there by the first you meet;
Or in Finsbury's Park, where swing
The raptured maidens in a ring,
There met on a sweet summer's day
With Innocence to romp and play—

M 2

Allusion which may some disdain,
But still a picture to remain
In my own private gallery,
Where will long sport my fantasy;
For mirth angelic there did flow,
Though whence it came they might not know.
So when we're sad by memory
We're gladden'd still by what we see,
Which proves that when some disappear,
The heav'nly bowers still are near
To many passing, as were they,
All through an Empyræan ray,
Not yet seen wholly, Heav'n's own glade,
Or else these others would have stay'd;
But still analogy is here,
And to that brightness are they near.
Youth dreads to lose the present hour,
So joyful is to him its power.
One drop upon his lips can be
An ocean's wide immensity
Of gladness which no future needs,
Towards which in mind he seldom speeds.
The radiant splendours of our East
Make for the young this life a feast;
And walking by themselves alone
They find now Eden is their own.

CANTO VIII.

TO AGE.

If thus through Paradise man's youth can stray,
In age, "life's evening," open lies the way
To those clear fountains which the saints employ
Now immortality to quaff with joy.

In the void region where no light was known
To Virgil's hero " sad old age " was shown.
But here its path is luminous and gay,
While leading onwards to celestial day,
As when some great metropolis is near,
And proofs increasing on the road appear
In brilliant objects which surprise the view,
And yield impressions that are felt as new—
Fill'd with great wonder as we each survey,
And feel th' attraction of the mighty sway.

Empedocles did style age " evening's glow,"
And Aristotle also, as we know.
But Saint Augustine, to views higher drawn,
Compared it, with more justice, to the dawn,
To fair Aurora, harbinger of light,
Which the grave sage De Prelle observed was right.
For though at all years men can go astray,
And dark and wretched can be age's way,
Declining, as Camillus did of old,
Accusing gods and men with murmurs bold,

Of many still, 'twould be more true to say,
That age is usher of th' eternal day—
The sacred influence of light appears
To chase so wholly all their human fears.
See we a sire to whom such grace belongs,
That we might say, as in grave Dantesque songs,
" O wondrous virtue ! with such smiling thought,
Thus com'st thou from the world's great snare uncaught ? "
That face, denoting fulness of content,
Proclaims through what transfigured shapes he went,
What glorious visions hover'd at his side,
How sweet had been his way through regions wide.
It is, in truth, that all the while his heart
Had seen of blessëd Paradise a part,
That he through everlasting spring had gone,
Had seen all beauty, life and joy in one,
The living sapphires, once our native land,
Surpassing all that seems to mortals grand;
It is that faith for him had not grown old,
Which made him Eden on this earth behold;
For Chrysostom observes faith waneth never;
And so, though Time he sees, he lives for ever.

But let us follow man thus walking free,
Beholding round him Heav'n's felicity,
Link'd in a golden chain, to Heav'n the earth,
The human victories, the angel's mirth.

And first, with constant labours never sad,
With mental or corporeal blithe and glad,
His industry itself attracts him on,
Till all life's troubles seem now past and gone.
Our wise old Friar Bacon still will " hold
That young folk are more slow to learn than old."
He " was prepared to prove it too," he said,
" And if he fail'd he would lay down his head."
Examples the conviction from him[1] wrung
That aged men learn'd much quicker than the young.
Such was Luc d'Achery in days of yore,
And Beaugendre, and countless scholars more;
Like Montfaucon and D'Andilly, who toil'd
At works from which the young might have recoil'd,
And Angelo and Titian, who beheld,
While both a bright, immortal pencil held,
Beauty's perfection in each noble face,
That their aged hands unwearied still would trace.
De Prelle depicts the sweetness of old age
In busy life, and that at every stage,
In civil, governmental, learnëd life,
Political and public, with its strife,
And shows, when Christian, how it hears the call
Of that which sanctifies and blesses all.
And then, grown wise by deep experience long,
Its flight towards bliss would suit Urania's song;

---

[1] Opus tert. c. 20.

If it were not far truer still to say,
Already that this bliss around it lay.
Then it holds light traditional for others,
Which neither cloud nor wind disturbs nor smothers;
For time has been its master, at whose feet
It sees the Truth Divine which makes all sweet.
Escaped from this life's snares, 'tis sure to see
The path that leads through true felicity;
Or rather, at that happiness arrived,
It reaps a rapture that has all survived.
A mental glory through its mind will range
Which, ne'er to pass, accompanies its change.
For now enlarged conceptions move its soul;
And kindness grows with instinct of the whole.
It views things on the side of nature more;
And that throws open wide a mystic door;
For nought is so mysterious unto man
As nature, so call'd, with its boundless span.
And schemes of men most learnëd and expert
Can never such an influence exert,
As thoughts disjointed that like springs will flow
From the vast depths where things unnamed will grow.
Reason will cast her nets, her webs will spin,
But age discards them for what's found within.
Reason gets oft entangled with her toil;
A doubt of false translation much can spoil.
A date, a letter, wrong interpretations
Can lead to some portentous aberrations.

But Nature, that to conscience must apply,
Will find, while systems crumble down and die,
What tends to elevate, make fair, excuse,
Not to degrade, and blacken, and abuse;
For, after all, when things thus age will sound
The fairest are most oft the deepest found.
So from mistrust, misgivings, doubts, and fears,
Age, less inclined to blame, most free appears.
And then, besides, for it the cheerful eye
That views all mortals destined to be high.
It seeks to level upwards, not below—
Downwards, like those who make a greater show;
It loves to raise, to comfort, and to bless,
All social sorrows truly to redress.
It learns with sense of certainty to track
The steps of men in errors far, far back;
" It understands their ignorance, and then,"
As Coleridge said, " it understands the men."
But kindness and indulgence will draw down
A bliss which angels even here will crown;
For tolerance and charity are one,
Inseparable, let what may be done;
And charity, with all her saintly train,
Sends back to Eden's joys our race again.

A certain Isabella, as they say,
Would once 'gainst Saint Theresa have her way.
A Saint herself, she later did deplore
Those contradictions which did grieve her sore.

To her, they say, Theresa came when dead,
And of these self-reproaches only said,
" Sigh no more, Isabella, sigh no more,
Nor think of what once pass'd in days of yore ;
For some things, let me tell you, that are here
To me far different do now appear."
And doubtless, adds the Priest who tells the tale,
That difference with Mercy will prevail.
Old age, thus half in Heav'n, has now to say
Somewhat like this in Saint Theresa's way.
It is not certain when our spirits sink,
That Heav'n thus of ourselves and deeds will think.
Age, doubtless, leaves the curtain half undrawn,
But round its head already glows the dawn.

Retractions e'en it often has to make
To favour others, or for truth's own sake.
" Its apples are then ripe," as Accius said,
When to another his own lines were read.
Pacuvius thought them sour and somewhat hard ;
When this similitude adduced the Bard,
To show that when a genius would endure,
Like his, it only later grows mature.
No longer has it an Olympian nod ;
It must grow kind, for it would be like God.
Its eyes are fix'd on the eternal sheen ;
It numbers hours only when serene,
Like that old dial which the monks had placed,
Upon whose column these sweet words were traced.

So blessings, not a curse, it will invoke;
And human follies ne'er can it provoke.
It has no hate, no threats, no withering scorn;
For loving all it feels that it was born.
On others' sins it cannot act the spy,
But with them laden to the cross 'twill fly.

Anticipations, too, belong to age,
With streams of hope which might all thirst assuage.
Forwards, not backwards, looking is its way;
And that alone explains the whole we say.
No morbid counting of regretted years
In such a happy mortal e'er appears;
As when degraded old men ever cry,
" Alas! we are not young; that time's gone by!"
Base, stupid words, discouraging, insane,
As if our souls were ever on the wane!
He says, " Consorting with the books that last
Exceeds all thinking on a time that's past;"
For, like Guevara, who this counsel gave,
He plays and laughs, while formal fools look grave.
While still 'tis beauty that attracts him on,
Of which the love for him is never gone;
And ever must he feel that to be loved
Himself is not a wish to be reproved;
Sage Roger Bacon says that most men die
Much sooner than demands necessity,

And that old age comes quicker than was meant
By God, who made man not with that intent[1].
He left in manuscript a formal page,
Entitled "On Retarding of Old Age[2]."
In fact, a man of many years may say
That still for him the charms of youth will stay.
The Nymphs, though not immortal known in song,
Do live, he will remind you, very long;
And he who loves ideas sweet and pure
Finds vital strength that will no less endure.
And so he sees around him beauty shed,
And is to God, who truly loves him, led—
That Friend of friends, and Comrade of his heart
In its most secret, tender, human part,
Who only has the right to count his days,
Since with him love that crown'd them ever stays;
And He alone their fruits or blights should tell,
To whom they owe whate'er with them was well.
Yes, to Him only should their faults be shown,
Who alone pardon'd, when the sum was known.
And 'tis to Him that men their sins lay bare
When kneeling low before the man of prayer.

But walking thus with such a comrade, friend,
'Tis Paradise already ne'er to end,
As when the sun in gorgeous splendour sinks,
And hill or plain its purple radiance drinks,

---

[1] Opus tert. c. 12.
[2] De retardatione senectutis.

The very dust, as upwards it will fly,
Becoming golden, like th' effulgent sky.
So earth for aged man blends into the sheen
Of the eternal garden that is seen,
Where Love and Freedom all renew'd will grow,
And streams of Paradise crystalline flow.
"Vitam futuri sæculi," he sings,
And to soar farther still expands his wings;
Since e'en through Eden though he seems to stray,
He travels as by night, and hopes for day.
All joy he thinks progressive, as he flies
To other gardens where he never dies.
Though still enraptured with the purple lawn,
His chief attraction is the golden dawn.
The earth to him half-hid is fraught with rest;
But he looks upwards, and the sky seems best.
That vast cerulean, starry, boundless cope
Makes all joys fade but those of deathless hope.
Dark ground, the approaching light, one picture fair—
'Tis Heav'n's own gates, and, oh, he would be there!

But now to what is general return,
Nor longer with a special age sojourn.

CANTO IX.

BY FRIENDSHIP.

Then, lo! another passage opens here,
Which shows on earth bright Heaven can be near.
    Forsooth, like Heav'n is Friendship's voice,
    And nought can mankind more rejoice.
    Which Senuesse e'en did prove,
    Seeing how friends their friends could love,
    As Horace, Virgil, with the rest,
    Who there became Muræna's guest.
    What love heroic in the tender cry
    Of Horace to Mæcenas standing nigh!
    " Why break my heart with such laments?
    No, die before me Heav'n prevents
    Thee, the far dearest, fondest part,
    As well thou knowest, of my heart.
    Without thee what have I to own?
    Or what should I do here alone?
    I have not sworn an idle oath;
    Depart we shall the same day both,
    Together go, yes, go we must,
    Like comrades who each other trust;
    Still wandering forwards, hand-in-hand,
    Still onwards to the sombre strand.
    No dreaded fabled monsters tear
    Me from thy side, though all be there—
    Though hundred-handed Gyas show,
    And horrible Chimæras glow.

Nought our two souls shall separate,
Please Justice and our common Fate!"

But take we life in each detail around,
And see what on this path is ever found.
Oh, 'tis Heav'n on earth to see
Friendship breathing mirth on thee!
Friendship that will sit or walk
With us, join in pleasant talk—
Serious or familiar things,
Such as oft your poet sings,
Hints or memories, a jest;
There the heart will find sweet rest.
Gladness has a jewel bright—
Friendship, nought more, cheers the sight.—
Gem that my D'Esgrigny knows—
Gem that Montague bestows.
" As thyself, love thou thy friend,
And unto my laws attend "—
Who spoke these words? who thus did call?
It was the Maker of us all.
Friendship's mirror is a glass
O'er which e'en Apostles pass;
For Saint Paul had friends far more
Than are counted in our store,
Special and beloved most dear,
As from letters doth appear.
Peter—he of Blois—has said,
" Friendship men to God has led;

For the rich it is a crown;
Riches for the lowest down;
Exiles find it native land;
With it can the weakest stand;
Life," he adds, " 'tis for the dead;
Heav'nward men by it are sped."
Many realized this rest,
As old annals can attest.
Mychomer the Monk is there,
With Saint Germain of Auxerre.
"One half of my soul," said he,
"In old Senateur I see."
Benedict and Sigfrid lay
Face to face, and pass'd away;
Bede says, " Kissing, so they pass'd,
Heav'n around them to the last."
We may also here remark
Benedict the Patriarch,
With Servandus in his sight,
All around him bathed in light.
Then Baronius felt the same
When Tarugi to him came.
So Paulinus, Alcuin,
Soar'd both above the world's din,
As did Charlemagne when near
Aquileia's prelate dear.
What was Eloi's brightest store?
Desiderius of Cahors.
Stray'd through Eden Dagobert,
When he saw his Sigebert.

Ives de Chartres so did wend,
Worcester's Samson for his friend.
For no seas could then divide
Those whose hearts were side by side.
Solon would at first refuse
Foreigners for friends to choose.
" Friendships are best found at home,"
Said the sage. So still might roam
Anacharsis, when he sought
Return for the love he brought—
Granted only when his wit
Caused the sage to deem him fit.
But such bars were never found
Where one faith ope'd every ground,
Yielding friendships that were true,
Such as Christian ages knew.
Sidonius found Heav'n's joy in youth,
Simplicius loving him with truth.
On Ommatius he does call,
" In whom Christ," he says, " gives all."
Amis and Amille were found
Straying thus through blissful ground,
   In that most ancient mystery,
   Of friendship's great felicity;
   Which fact I cite since e'en romance
   Must thus through Paradise advance.

O Cambridge, Alma Mater! who but thou
Should'st add an instance from experience now?

While friendship on this earth can still remain,
Turning to thee our search will not be vain.
For nature unsophisticated stays
With thee to sweeten all thy daily ways.
Thy sons are seldom stiffen'd into stone;
With thee no formal contradiction grown;
For no false, gloomy guides, as elsewhere, try
To pass off pride for truth, and manners high;
And vessels out at sea are safe far more
Than those, steer'd wrong, left stranded on the shore.
Ah! suffer me of some to tell and sing
Whose kindness in time past now aids my wing,
Assail'd by voices from the crowd that cry,
" Contempt is due to bards who think to fly."
Thorpe was exact, enthusiastic Hare;
Solid was Rose, and Sedgwick past compare,
For honest spirit and for noble mind,
The type of manhood, brave, and frank, and kind.
Hare! shall I only name him in my song?
Right's fearless champion, pulverizing Wrong,
In depth a Plato, for the weakest mild,
A guide with Sages, and with youths a child—
Hare was a joy you thought could never end,
A light for judgments, and for hearts a friend.
Wordsworth was learnëd, timid, for delay,
Though conscious life was speeding fast away;
Well skill'd on any course the prize to win,
Yet still regretting he could not begin.
For little talents must with speed be shown,
While genius waits, and passes hence unknown.

"The man of promise" here may live in shade,
To bloom forth glories elsewhere being made.
Valpy was curious, critical, though shy,
In mien still lowly, while his heart was high.
A classic fancy was to Shadwell given,
To Whewell all the knowledge under Heav'n.
Famed or obscure, I name them altogether—
Master or student differ'd not a feather;
For Whewell had the virtues of a boy,
Though mental strength did oft the proud annoy;
And Romilly's or Peacock's smile would seem
E'en to their pupils like true Friendship's dream.
Grave Porter would leave fluxions for his friend;
And Bagshaw's love with life would only end.
Oh that I could pourtray in worthy strain
Worsley's bright fancy, and the sense of Bayne!
Elmslie, who Fielding's very spirit owns,
So tuned to echo all its sweetest tones!
Aristophanic Barnes so skill'd to show
How Grecian wit in English verse should flow;
Or Sidney Walker, whom Miltonian prose
Employ'd translating till his life's swift close,
Timid, distrustful, all whose doubts had flown
From mental sickness, as his friends would own.
Kemble's good-nature, Churchill's pluck and fire.
Than Talbot's Science some would more admire.
Then Darby was the model of a knight;
Whatever Glennie said was always right—
Whom Science fed, yet who would not less stray
With drawing, music, charming cares away.

Flamank from Eton was a swimmer bold,
For whom the Cam in winter was not cold;
With whom for three years I did breast its flow,
When ice would float and wild white tempests blow,
When fields were flooded (which delighted more),
And yellow torrents mined each green isle's shore,
Ah! Friendship midst the willows then was warm,
While braving icebergs, sleet, or rain, or storm.
Poor Hastings! an Adonis in his youth,
Aye practised goodness, piety, and truth;
Mansel had pluck'd all flow'rets that e'er grew
In English letters to present to you;
Sage Kindersley would play each gentle part;
And Kingdon brought you sunshine in his heart;
Shaw, that from Westminster to us had flown,
Had guileless speech pure Innocence might own;
And Murray, pensive, skill'd on the guitar,
Beyond the earth in mind would wander far;
Bayley was gentle, even while afloat
And ruling eight men in our far-famed boat,
Of whom two, Blane and Mayo, proved to be
Heroes in war, renown'd for chivalry.
Phillips, deep-read in mediæval books,
Had Heav'n around him, Heav'n in his looks;
Praed could find merit, be it e'er so low,
And e'en on Digby some kind lines bestow;
Spenser—my hand too coarse should fear to paint
The English noble, and the Christian saint—
There was not one whose presence did not bring
For dulness Fairyland, for Heav'n a wing.

Friendship's wants no less can lead
To th' Elysian fields with speed;
And, in truth, we often find
That to earth 'tis not confined,
That complete it cannot be
If no farther we can see.
What are friends in London life,
With its dissipated strife?
Just the same we can behold,
As in the past years of old.
Knots which but the worldly fit,
By their own hands are unknit.
Oh, the joys that pass all measure
In true Friendship's honest pleasure!
But how seldom now can meet
Those true friends who friends would greet!
Who now, in a fragrant bower,
With his friend would stop an hour?
Grand inventions often bring,
With some solaces, a sting;
As Guevara said, " 'Tis thus
News will sometimes come to us
In one day, for which we'd wait
Rather thirty, past debate."
While they make the ill come fast,
They forbid the good to last.
So these means for changing place
Friendship's pleasures oft efface.
Railways, though no poet sings,
Fix on Friendship swallows' wings.

All must fly and pass away;
Warmest friends with you can't stay.
Possibly to seek their nest,
Flying there you think were best.
But who knows the hour precise
When to see him? what device
Can now be framed by any one
To find a friend not " out " and gone?
Manners that old Florence loved
Would now only be reproved.
Early, or too late, would be
Simply rude vulgarity.
At the intermediate hours
Always some obstruction lowers.
Luncheons, absence through sheer pride—
All these things will friends divide,
Leaving them with nought to do
But, in French, to cry " *blanc chou* "—
Words, you can perceive, all quaint,
Disappointed hopes to paint.
It is own'd in town around,
Friends at home are never found;
For all leave the house each day
When each would his visit pay—
Clever and ingenious plan
Ne'er to meet a friendly man.
They converse with seas asunder,
For inventions create wonder.
America and India find
 Words sent from London that seem kind—

Flash'd in moments, as they dance—
Or from Germany and France.
Mark you, it is words they send;
For with them must converse end.
Send language of the heart and eye
Can never they, nor yet a sigh;
Nor indeed for them is lost
Aught when they have paid the cost.
Besides, who sends what he has not,
When real friendship is forgot?
So friends in an adjoining street
Live much too far for them to greet.
Those whom antipodes divide,
'Twixt whom oceans are not wide,
May expect to greet each other—
Not so neighbours and a brother.
These for ever live apart;
Cables are not for the heart.
Science can transport, appal;
When that's done we think it all.
Friendship fond our age would tire;
It must live upon a wire.
Friendship therefore here must be
Nought except a mockery.
Poor Ausonius, in his times,
Uses words would suit these rhymes.
" Rocks," he says, " will answer man,
Yes, caverns and forests can,
Rivulets that flow with speed,
Trees that bees of Hybla feed,

Willows on the river's bank,
Waving pines that dews have drank;
All converse as with the wind—
While Paulinus is unkind,
Obstinately silent yet,
For his friend he does forget."
Leuthericus of Sens no less
Hears Fulbert the same grief express.
To-day friends are to many known,
But whom to-morrow they disown.
Public life can thus efface
Private and familiar grace.
" Hearts of old," 'tis said, " gave hands;"
Hands, not hearts, our world commands.
Such is our new heraldry,
Such the blazon that we see!
" Let's meet seldom till the end—
God be with you!" says each friend.
Friendship true must needs have vent,
Countless ways none can prevent.
But what you can smoothly cover
Must be weak for any other.
On what finger now you will
Place your ring. It can fulfil
All your purpose by a show,
Though no nerve leads to and fro.
Only those who would impart
To another their whole heart
Need to fix it on the next
To the little one annex'd,

Whence 'twas thought a nerve most fine
Reach'd my heart, to make it thine.
Place it where all see it well;
Of nought else it has to tell.
" What is Friendship?" Alcuin asks;
" Likeness real, and not masks."
" Grandees ne'er should see each other,
If they would not Friendship smother;"
So says Philip de Commines,
Who the great had often seen.
If 'tis so, th' electric wire
Is for Princes to admire—
Be that true or be it not,
Thoughts of friendship are forgot.
Such is now that ancient port
To which vainly we resort.
Life advancing, men discover
Friends can't do much for each other.
Now and then an hour beguile,
More to hope 'tis not worth while.
Many you perhaps have known;
Grave things you must meet alone.
Face to face with them you'll be,
None in sight to stand with thee.
Friends to aid you stay too far;
Sole with Fortune, there you are!
This is when they do their best;
What is it with all the rest?
Rising, they will wait on you,
Sinking, that would never do.

They accept your invitation,
If accordant with their station;
But to follow you in mind,
Is what they can never find.
And then in hours sad will they
Drop off one by one away.
Impotent they needs must be,
When the soul feels misery;
They can yield, I fear at best,
But a sunny moment's rest.
For you living, they're "the town,"
Dead, they'll have you well nail'd down.
Buried, they've no time to spare;
Choose your grave; not one goes there.
All this sophists will explain,
Proving that complaints are vain.
Analytic ages grow
Careless about friendship's glow.
Friendship, too, has had its day,
Just like poetry, they say.
Bootless is it to complain,
So look elsewhere—there remain.
Heav'n and earth you'll find will meet,
When at last you choose retreat.

Friendship, nathless, must exist,
Though its sweets we may have miss'd.
Classic pages still can tell
How its pleasures all were well.

For Gracchus to his Blosius bound,
Rheginus with Servilius found,
And Lælius with Scipio,
Can thus the ancient friendship show.
Agrippa and Augustus e'en
Such true familiar friends are seen.
If but Cicero were left
We should not be quite bereft
Of a sign that love must be
Real, true felicity,
Such as Aylward, too, did paint,
As a Christian and a saint;
Such as Italy once knew,
Picus and Ficinus drew.
But since changed is now its fate,
Look we to a higher state,
Where its sweets will all be found,
Gather'd from this nether ground.
Since the times are out of joint,
Friendship will now to Heav'n point,
Where no distance is too great,
Such as friends will here create,
Where we may converse above
With the spirits here we love.
Yes, it leaves us Heav'n in sight,
Not as light'ning leaves the night,
Starless, comfortless, and drear,
But with those we best love near.

Still friendship, binding poor to poor,
Even with us can now endure.

In Friendship—not from pride of life,
And growing up with all its strife,
But from the humble root of love—
Men can see Heav'n from above
Descending with its blissful rays,
To bless and sweeten all their days;
Sitting silent, side by side,
Heart from heart will nought divide;
Straying onwards, hand in hand,
Angel-life they understand;
Greenwood tree and mossy seat
Witness how they often meet;
Or they watch the gliding stream
Rapt in an Elysian dream—
" Words " can hardly interchange
Those whose hearts through Eden range;
But they feel, and gaze around,
Where is Heav'n already found;
For the silent heart is more
Than wit's vaunted brightest store.
Friendship loves equality,
Makes the poor and rich agree,
Levels pride with its disdain,
Finishes the world's long reign,
Bridles all the manners vile
Which the tameless will beguile,
Adviseth well. That debt paid,
Comes Divinity to aid;
Thinking love for a true friend
Never can with this life end;

Loves the person, as in God,
On each path it ever trod.
Seeks what death cannot destroy,
So secures eternal joy
Even on this earth begun—
All its sweets for ever won.
What it wants and what it yields
Lead us thus to Eden's fields.
Its wants wing us to the sky ;
Its gifts bring down from on high
Heav'n's own life commencing now
'Neath each bloom of greenwood bough.

As when you travel near some fair, bright spot
   Where you sat happy once, long years ago,
With some one absent now, but ne'er forgot,
   And all reminds you of the one you know ;
When you think of nothing but a mind—
Like what in Fairy Bowers children find—
A living person who did make the whole,
   Immense enchantment, an ideal joy ;
The constant charms thus being from a soul
   In which was nought that could the heart annoy ;
Not from the seat or grass on which you roll'd,
Nor purple woods that cover'd all the wold,
Nor villas sparkling in the morning air,
   Nor flowers, nor slopes that deck'd the verdant
     ground—
So in the strange, inexplicable fair
   That steals our hearts when nought explain'd is
     found—

'Tis from the land unseen, where all is well,
That came the sweet, unearthly, joyous spell!
 A minstrel in the days of yore
 Might here one short tale from his store
 Adduce, to speed us to the end,
 And show where we can meet a friend.
 "There lived," saith he, "a gentleman
 (I name him not, although I can),
 Then aged, and who had travell'd much;
 And now there still are many such.
 But he was full of plain good sense,
 Without illusions or pretence;
 So that through all the country round
 The best adviser he was found.
 A certain knight, it chanced one day,
 Came to consult him in that way.
 'Prud'homme,' said he (and I must tell
 The word he used it sounds so well,
 And has such meaning wide, profound,
 That no equivalent is found)—
 'Prud'homme, I find just nothing here
 To make this neighbourhood right dear
 To me, who wish a happy life,
 Far from the faintest trace of strife.
 There's nought to fix me in this spot
 Where I do oft lament my lot.
 To what land, tell me, should I speed,
 Where I can satisfy my need?'
 The old man answer'd, 'Then repair
 To some new land with no one there

You thus to trouble on your way,
And against whom you've nought to say.'
' But if I should be follow'd still,
And only find a change of ill ? '
Then, said the other, ' Thither steer
Where all men will have you to fear.'
The knight then said, ' But if there be
No cause there found for fearing me ? '
The wise Prud'homme then gravely said,
As though some deep thought fill'd his head,
' Seek then a land where you will find
Those who will wish to love your mind—
In short, to love you, that is all,
Howe'er for happiness you call.'
Then, with a sigh, the other said,
' If thither now I should be sped,
And there be none to love me there ? '
' Ah, then to Heav'n you must repair,'
Replied the sire, ' for there alone
Your heart finds echo of its tone [1].' "
Then in Virgilian words might say
The wanderer thus left astray,
" ' There is your love, your country fair,
Apollo bids you hasten there."

---

[1] Le Grand, "Contes et Romans Anciens" (tom. iv. 185).

CANTO X.

BY LOVE.

Now at the sweet word "Love" my lyre will sound,
As if a more congenial theme were found.
For 'tis a law, as poets even say,
That every heart must give itself away.
Yea, all things here below must somewhat yield,
The air, the earth, the forest, and the field.
'Tis dew, or fruits, or peace it will impart;
But no gift equals that of one true heart.

Methinks the bard of Greece bids us rejoice,
When singing these words with melodious voice.
" Horses have marks by which we always trace
Their kind, and use, their nation, and their race;
The Parthian men can any one soon know
By the tiaras which they always show.
But I immediately can lovers tell
From knowing their interior lines so well;
For a peculiar trait they have of soul,
A certain fine-mark which proclaims the whole."
Responsive to the colours of the scene
Where an aussonian beauty pours its sheen,
I now would fling distrust and fear away,
And with such careless joy sing as I may.
Here, man's proud opposition oft will fade,
As if o'erpower'd by the myrtle shade;

Nor will true happy fields be farther, though
We haunt the scenes where Grecian waters flow—
Bright Paphos, and the clear Laconian coast
Where fair Cythera still enchanteth most.
For love is potent to resist the sway
Of all the social thraldom of our day ;
To ancient trophies never yield will he,
Or care for shields and crests of heraldry.
He flies beyond conventional restraint,
And, unlike friendship, urges no complaint.

> What surpasses human thought?
> Love—for all the rest is nought.
> What's the world without that spell?
> What are all its raptures? tell.
> Gardens, fountains, yield but anguish,
> Hearts with all such pleasures languish ;
> Golden palaces appear
> Soulless desolation drear.
> What surpasses human thought?
> Love—for all the rest is nought.

Oh, marvel not, but pensively reflect,
That God from man does only love expect.
" Th' eternal wisdom," as our Greville sings,
" His strength and reason counts as minor things."
'Tis love, and only love He seeks from man ;
Since love, of all our good still holds the van,
Which every thought of ours will rule and guide,
Maugre our strength, our reason, and our pride.

Not, sooth, the lowest end of life, our love
Sees Paradise not distant up above,
Close spreading round here its Elysian shade,
For which he feels by Nature he was made;
And, " without error still," as Dante sings,
" The love that's natural will feel no stings."
While Love exemptions hath, as lovers know,
His look alone brings Heav'n on earth below,
By means of things unto our nature lent,
Which God alone could furnish and invent.
The son of Theseus would have gold prescribed,
And e'en to Jove the love of it ascribed.
But love, of planetary light possest,
Turns pale, and quite discolours all the rest.
The memory of love can cheer alone,
And draw from some poor heart Lamartine's tone—
All proudly, humbly utter'd with a sigh,
" God will forgive me, since once loved was I."

Love finds upon his bright and fragrant way
No pathless thickets, that his feet can stay
From passing ever to what's fair and right,
Whose beauteous blossoms charm his ravish'd
    sight.
The love of Beauty leads man ever on
To joys celestial which his soul has won.
How often, pensive, has he fled the crowd
In trees and flowers all his mind to shroud,
Thinking that they e'en cognizant must be
Of his own love and true felicity!

As if 'twere whisper'd to the woods and bowers
With signs of gratulation from the flowers,
Which never love divine will drive away
Displeased, that with the wing'd boy he should play;
Since love leads up to Heav'n, a way, a guide,
And ne'er is blamed unless by human pride.
Detach'd from self by means of love, we know
That self is never caught again below.
Love knows a heart once given to another
You never can again in life recover
So as to be yours become alone ;
That other fled, the heart to Heav'n is flown.
Such the beginning, such the end of love,
One and the same for earth and Heav'n above.
For " Love that virtue begs, and virtue grants,"
With selfish, secret wishes never pants.
" 'Tis woman's love," (disprove this no one can)
As Lily saith, " which maketh e'en the man."
So well might Fabius Maximus decide
To bear with lovers, and to take their side.
No dark obstructions which ill roots reveal,
As vain and blind ambition, can conceal
From man or woman that impressive face
Of truth, in which all happiness we trace;
For Love refuses not, will ne'er deny,
And so far soars to bounteous Heav'n nigh.
Urania even will not scorn to sing
Such common Love, or plume for him her wing—
If that can be styled common which is rare
As love must be—no egotism there.

That which by God Himself was first devised,
Methinks by man should hardly be despised.
What o'er all human art will fly above
Consorts with Heav'n on earth ; and that is Love,
Who has his own bright spreading wings to soar,
Which than all tutor'd breath will serve him more.
So woman seldom likes professions loud ;
She rather seeks her thoughts within to shroud.
"Say, do you love me ? " asks her lover true ;
She only whispers then, " You know I do,"
Words that convey a meaning more profound
Than what from lips of men will often sound,
Though like a Melville or Léonce they burn
With high conceits that common youth would spurn,
Which should be heard by waterfalls and rocks,
And not by one who words bombastic mocks.
" Would you forgive me," asks the swain, " if you
All my grave faults or keen misfortunes knew ? "
" Forgive you first," she answers, " now will I,
Then hear them afterwards, so kiss, good-bye."
Men oft deceive, not often damsels fair ;
In them the crime of falsehood is most rare.
'Tis Ovid says it, in harmonious verse,
The truth of which attests the universe ;
For woman-haters are exceptions few,
Whose feign'd experience cannot hide the true.
Oh, give me those who have no wish to vie
With clever adepts whose discourse is sly !

> Though Lizzie opens not her lips,
> 'Tis near her one Ambrosia sips;
> Though to speak not be her rule,
> Near her, each wit seems a fool;
> Though her love were all her wit,
> Near her I'd for ever sit.

But oft what men propose is only show,
That all the world their proudest things may know,
As "things" they count those who hold foremost place
In the self-love that's stamp'd upon their face;
And so, though these are last in their esteem,
Magnificent to all eyes they must seem.
Unlike that Demades, who told his son
When he his mother's love and hand had won,
Their next-door neighbour hardly knew of aught,
So little then were Hymen's splendours sought—
Perhaps no symptom of a foolish age,
Though men who blame it are now thought more sage.
At least the joys of which I sing will glide
With not more noise than yields our river's tide,
As gentle and as silent as the stream,
Oft the sole witness of a summer's dream,
As much unthought of elsewhere or unknown
As is the lily floating there alone.

But let us hear some frank Idyllic bard,
Who ventures Fashion's thraldom to discard,
Like honest Amyot to leave distrust,
And simply sing just as a lover must;

Who ne'er expects to meet an evil eye,
Sinistrous visage, sign of danger nigh,
But here, as with a true friend left alone,
Love's early raptures to describe and own,
And like a finish'd miniature to paint
What haters make a subject of complaint;
Who, if they could ordain all things on earth,
Would leave it without love, or joy, or mirth,
Or any bliss to all the world not known,
Or aught spontaneous but self-love alone,
Or circumstance exceptional, although
No danger thence to aught revered could flow;
Or sportive mornings or a pleasant day,
Forbid by "What would this or that one say?"
Or rural walks, or seats in woodbine bowers,
Or aught recalling Eden and its hours,
Or strolls at dusk, or 'neath the noon-tide sun,
Or any harmless, ancient, human fun,
Or flowers of spring, or fruits of autumn fair,
Or slopes to rest on, breathing perfumed air,
Or summer eves, by stream or fragrant shore,
Or hearts united, peaceful, which is more.

O breath of summer's eve how sweet thou art,
When love has touch'd to tune the human heart!
As 'neath one tree in twilight hour you sat
And hark'd the birds, and held as lightsome chat;
One slope received both on its lushy bank
When wearied down upon the weeds you sank;

While the sun, radiant with a sweet farewell,
Spread far his evening beams o'er shaded dell;
Or later, as you caught the far, far gleams
From cottage windows whence a candle streams
Across the level woodland, till the light
Recall'd our Shakspear's simile from night.
And yet, this Bard will add, still sweeter seems
The dawn that follows with its golden beams!
Ah! with what rays, cries he, that morn will shine
When yesterday another's heart was thine!
The Real seems the music of a Lyre,
'Tis the Miltonian touch, and that heard nigher.
Oh, then the earth with Eden can compare,
As coming forth you greet Aurora there,
And find how all things to true love belong,
Are tuneable as sylvan pipe or song.
The stream-side Inn, he'll sing, the bank with flowers,
The air embalm'd amidst the willow bowers,
The whole a scene of pastoral delight,
With nothing left but Fancy's forms in sight;
He'll sing some fairy, with a brilliant wand,
Who makes each part with Love to correspond.
He'll sing that primal peace, without offence,
Interior voices calm, without pretence;
That innate image of our happy time,
Of which the summer bringeth back the clime,
Which in the human memory will last
Like a primæval bliss that all surpass'd.
He'll sing the love which earthly bounds will scorn,
For nothing finite feeling itself born.

Though still conversant with the lowly here,
Though noblest, humblest, and though common dear.
What's seen and heard is small, familiar, trite,
Though fraught each moment with a new delight.
The least details Love's novelties reveal,
He'll sing the Host who brings the early meal—
His stately ways to you familiar grown,
As if the house itself were all your own.
The smallest items he will paint with care;
He'll sing the glance cast up to windows there;
He'll sing the tawny plains, the mists that rise,
Foreshowing heat of later noon-tide skies,
The distant reeds that quiver in the stream,
And cause long lines of light o'er shades to gleam;
He'll sing the birds now waken'd as before,
The charm that issues from the trellised door,
When she who makes a Paradise around,
Gay as a lark is seated near you found,
Unskill'd to practise aught but Nature's part,
Dear as the ruddy drops that warm your heart.
Yes, he will sing details for artist's eyes,
Which those who love like you will not less prize—
Things that in Love's law have long pass'd for good,
Though oft as reasonless misunderstood,—
To-day, as yesterday, the boat again,
The tall green rushes and the sultry plain,
The strange impressions of the potent spell
Of which the charm no human words can tell.
The tree whose thick dark leaves the Inn will shroud
With chant of tuneful birds resounding loud,

As if beneath a vault through which they fly,
Where they and you may outward things defy—
A pillar'd shade, high over-arch'd, where night
Will seem to reign for ever, quenching sight;
Though still below and straight before you lies
The sparkling tide, become to lover's eyes,
The whispering stream that glides along so near,
From whose soft murmurs they have nought to fear;
He'll sing the objects evening hid from sight,
Now seen distinctly with the morning light,—
Where ruby Vesper placed one purple line,
The weir, the lock brought out like gems to shine,
All seeming changed by aspects of the sun,
While your enchantment is each hour begun;
The golden morn, with new, fresh pleasures ranged,
Alone your love, and Love's sweet dream un-
    changed,—
These are the items of that rapture new,
Intense, as if with Eden in your view.
But why proceed, since only those can know
Who love like you, what here he'd strive to show.
None fully know what's felt in Heav'n above;
But this we know, our joys are joys of love.
Here, in brief space, they needs must speed away;
There, by eternal laws they ever stay.
Ah well, as Calderon sublimely sings,
Such love, though low on earth, will ask no wings;
For while a little world man has been call'd,
The heav'nly world has woman oft forestall'd;

Since woman, whom upon this earth we see,
Of Heav'n is now a true epitome.
So sang the grave and peerless Bard of Spain,
With whose sweet words I'd grace my humble strain.
By love, she leads man to a sacred home,
From which, while love endures, he ne'er will roam.
" I once did believe in nothing," says a youth,
"Till woman did impart a sense of truth.
The sight of my betrothed, so true to me,
Woke in my soul a sense of dignity,
As what unto the human mind belong'd,
Which hitherto in me I felt was wrong'd.
Her love brought immortality to view,
And did my spirit and my heart renew.
No longer life on earth seem'd dark and drear;
I saw, I felt that Heav'n itself was near."
So love, with all its incidents that charm,
Protects our life, and will its foes disarm;
Leads through a flow'ry path that will surprise,
When, mounting thus, it reaches past the skies;
And man, while here on earth, such joy has found,
He is no more " a scorner of the ground."
Nay, (what serves more sweet Heav'n on earth to trace)
It makes us love the whole soft human race.
The love of one can scarce with faults agree,
When thus imparting truest charity.

Still nought more dearly shows us what's above
Than the deep sadness upon earth of love;

As oft as but the absent we must greet,
Though even this is found supremely sweet;
"As when you sit," the Bard will say, "and think,
And find your heart so wing'd it cannot sink,"
Recalling what we lately had in view,
Which memory will year by year renew.
Yet rays of yesterday you only see
In your mind's eye, a past felicity.
All that did charm the past, that memory hears,
Is fled already, to the eternal years—
The boat, the sun, the evening by the stream
Exists for you but as a cherish'd dream.
Those joys so lively on the spangled shore
Return to you on earth perhaps no more.
But though the form should change the joy and peace,
May both be found elsewhere no more to cease;
For things so bright were never meant to die,
Though here from you they fled in infancy.
There must exist in presence true and bright
What here the mind alone may have in sight;
As when the poet cries, "In every place,
At every moment I behold thy face;
Sick or in health I equally am thine;"
But love like this partakes of the divine;
Since here 'tis but an image in the heart,
Seen, heard, enjoy'd, remember'd but in part.
But to remember so with no one nigh,
Is, as the Poet sings, to wish to die.

If age will love as fervently as youth,
Its love is part of this immortal truth,
That we for love, love without end, were made,
Though here our thoughts converse but with a
    shade;
And when of senile love rude men complain,
They only prove that they themselves are vain.
For all through life this path to Eden lies,
By love, with joy or sadness past the skies.

There are joys which no poet can tell;
    There are griefs no Muse can sing;
Visions there are that can throw a spell
Of conviction at once, that the whole is well,
    And to thoughts impart a wing.

For all love is a celestial air
    That comes fragrant down from Heav'n;
And it makes this earth so strangely fair
That all things a beautiful robe will wear,
    To each by its magic given.

Yes, earth can yield oft bright Eden's hour,
    As if on its shores begun,
And fairies with all their vaunted power,
Could never create such a blissful bower,
    As when that sweet land is won.

Its sorrows no less unfold that sheen;
    For then where do lovers turn,
Save to the bright walks in mind all seen,
Which e'en here have the true asylum been
    When earth's ground true hearts will spurn?

CANTO X.

What skills the great pains you 'ale below?
  Why so much trouble and fear?
All the false goods that they can bestow
Will pass like a shadow as years will flow;
  So love then—and disappear.

    Yes, nought of life will then remain,
    Save having loved; all else is vain.
    Sooth others may perhaps portray
    The object of a Poet's lay.
    For me it only can be given
    To show how she can draw down Heaven.
    Nought opens quicker those domains,
    Where Innocence with gladness reigns,
    Than the small, simple, ancient key,
    With which she touches you and me.
    Whate'er she wills to do or utter,
    Elysian zephyrs round her flutter.
    From nothing then will surely rise
    Fine Histories, with which nothing vies.
    Lovers, like Poets, never fear
    Rude, common objects to be near;
    The Types heroic they adore,
    Which only make them prized the more;
    Nor do they heed through what they fly,
    However low to soar on high.
    If in great cities be her home,
    'Tis through those quarters they would roam,
    Which morn or eve behold the lass,
    Unseen by them when she will pass.

'Tis seeing her, to hear their name,
Or that you likewise from them came;
And so, taking fire at the sound,
They fancy she herself is found.
Each street familiar to her eyes,
Will to them bright with beauty rise.
The cripple stretching forth his palms
All day, soliciting men's alms,
Seems to have some amends for woe,
Since she must pass him, as they know.
The horse-boy, though he use his spur,
Who often has been seen by her,
Will be esteem'd as having won
Her glance, though but a tradesman's son.
They envy, (shall I dare to own,
Some now are so fastidious grown,
That words familiar to the street
In Poems you must never meet,
Although they often softly rise
To sweetest lips, and none surprise?)
They envy lads, whose crossings clean,
By her approving must be seen.
Though mansions they may pass not by,
Some well-known corners see them nigh,
Drawn by a magic which defies
All that attracts true vulgar eyes.
Scorn if some will a vulgar name;
But Love knows nought of vulgar shame.
He envies them their signs, and stands,
(All this each lover understands).

Little cares he for all the wines
That tapsters offer at such signs.
Shakspear and Chaucer often named
The things of common life unblamed.
What will not projects serve to cloak?
He'll name " The Bell " or " Royal Oak."
'Tis solely, Nature is so sly,
That some one needs must pass them by;
And hence, he loves their name to hear,
Recalling one that is so dear;
Some business will he have, or make,
Compelling him that way to take;
Where he will loiter, wanting nought,
But quite contented with his thought.
The very pavement of the spot
Could tell how nothing is forgot;
The dogs that eye things from their door,
And boys whose staring vexeth more
Could tell it all, if only they
Would mix their sly remarks with play.
Not strange you'd think it, being so,
If what Love loves you were to know.

But speed to where a people lately raged,
And worse than civil wars have fiercely waged;
What is it then to see the maiden pass
Amidst the wild confusion's hideous mass!
Ah, what a contrast is the shelter'd home,
Whither she will, you think, so gladly roam!

The lover thinks, the spot that sees her smile
Must needs be Eden's garden for the while.
From Ruin's havoc, staring black and gaunt,
Where war has revell'd, or which rebels vaunt,
He is in mind transported to some p'ace
Where Nature reigns with her primæval grace,
Where faith and goodness have contrived to stay,
And social horrors are deem'd far away;
For while fierce citizens will wildly lower,
There he finds subjects of another power.
And when two hearts in one are so combined,
True peace in that small unity you find.
No times, no places then can quite exclude
The bliss which reigns without vicissitude.
When hearts united thus are constant found,
'Twill matter less the changes all around.
They make their own times, their own place, and world,
Howe'er the earth around them may be hurl'd.
To one another open, all the rest—
Is closed, shut out, while they alone are blest.
The sky for others may be overcast,
The time of joy for them is never past.
The looks of one will from the other draw
The same sweet fancy by a secret law;
The word of one that would express a thought,
Springs to the other's lips already brought,
The looks are words, the eye explains the heart,
Love will a language of his own impart;

And so this twofold and most happy life
Disdains the force of Revolution's strife;
At least the English lover thinks that thus
Must love assuage all ills that come to us.

  But say I still that love has woe,
  Though best of all things found below.
  Hard, not to love, although it be,
  'Tis hard to love, as all can see;
  But hardest yet of all will prove
  Misfortune in the course of love.
  Yes, let us hear the Greek of old,
  Whose fable these wounds best has told.

 " Love, once among the roses lay;
  A bee his finger stung;
 He thought with all that's sweet to play;
  But now his hands he wrung.

 " Loud then he cried, to Venus flew;
  'I perish!' was his cry;
 (As if Cythæra aught could do,)
  'I perish, and I die.

 "' A little serpent, wing'd, touch'd me,
  The rose-buds here among,
 Which rustic mortals call a bee,
  O look where I've been stung!'

 " She answer'd, 'If a small bee's sting
  Can cause thee so much woe,
 What think'st thou must those feel and sing
  Who thy keen arrows know?'"

P

Our chief joys are in memory,
A fanciful sweet reverie
Which draws and draws us to one spot,
To live on what is ne'er forgot—
The thought of some one lately nigh
Whose absence prompts the secret sigh.
The present is too oft allied
With fears, which Reason have defied;
As when, like Corinne, hearts will cry,
Oh, touch not future Destiny!
It scares us so, whene'er we would
As moulding it be understood,
As wishing to obtain still more
Than it now gives us from its store!
Oh, change nought in the present hour!
While happiness is in our power!
Yet, in the transports of this state
There's what the tongue does not relate—
What makes them yield unto the past,
When memory alone did last.
In either case, we must allow,
Love's triumph is not often now.
Th' ideal, then, will prove what's best,
And vague unquietness the rest.
In human love, while here below,
There's more, far more than mortals know.

Yet what of love we do know is sublime;
More would transcend the bounds of mind and time.

We know that it is one, yet varied ever,
Though we can seize the total of it never;
No more than men can all the tempest see,
Or view at once the sea's immensity.
We know that it develops in the heart
What forms its noblest and divinest part,
That nought brings forth, refines, or perfects more
The good that lies within it, as its ore,
That whatsoe'er the person be you love,
The love inspired will lift your heart above
All selfish interests, high above the world,
Though to perdition it would have you hurl'd.
Think you with love would woman soft compare
The carriage, jewels, that make idiots stare?
That what once pleased her, loving none and nought,
When loving now could occupy her thought?
This light from Eden puts out every flame,
However bright when first to her it came.
And then when clouds will gather, anger lower,
Say, what can stand before Love's mighty power?
The ancient tyranny of states may rage,
The pride of families may ape the sage,
But one poor Marguerite, or Marian then
Can yield examples to heroic men,
To prove that love yields martyrs for the sky,
And such as e'en Religion can supply;
For those who all renounce, and die for love,
Must reign for ever, since love reigns above.

Clear is the strain when words our thoughts convey
The certain knowledge of our little day;
Gently it flows and wafts along its stream
In smoothest numbers what we touch, not dream.
But when our words infinity would tell,
Ah, then the Muse finds broken all her spell;
Then clear distinctness seems to fly her lyre,
The less accordant as it soundeth higher.
No more in sounds monotonous you find
The whole completeness of a little mind.
In dissonance at least will toil along
The heavy structure of her labouring song;
Then inconsistent, vague, without an end,
Her course seems nowhere while the words still wend.
'Tis sounds abrupt, 'tis sentences that jar,
'Tis baffled sense that wanders like a star,
One moment casting unexpected light,
To vanish at the next in clouded night.
She struggles and falters, feels her power fade,
As if for singing love she was not made;
Theme far too high, and for an angel's tongue,
Not for a harp like ours by mortals strung.
For how could she sing God? and He, we know,
Is Love—Love in Heav'n as on earth below.

CANTO XI.

BY GOODNESS.

But now let us o'er rising lawns ascend,
And to the scenes of common goodness wend,
Involving an idea from its birth
Of what is most esteem'd by the whole earth;
Which none can love, as we are taught to do,
Without the consequence of pleasure too.
The ancient Spartans, as Valerius said,
Knew well that virtue could be sooner led
To luxury, or earth, as we may say,
Than luxury or earth can find the way
To virtue, yielding unto human minds
The bliss which man in fields Elysian finds;
And so 'tis proved, experience will attest;
Yet Goodness yields the passage shortest, best.
For instantaneously she opens wide
The doors which men from happiness divide.

    Sameness proves oft a hideous spell,
    Whose fountain is the deepest hell.
    But goodness and monotony
    Can ne'er together long agree.
    For goodness yields, but still to rise
    Victorious to her native skies.
    What interest can you ever take
    In those on whom no light will break?

When nothing bright can rise again,
The scenes of life must needs be vain—
Where happy changes can't be found,
Of strict necessity the ground
Must from the first reduce your play
To a mere sorrowful array
Of hopeless passages in view,
Which no skill'd bard would e'er renew.
In men who have retain'd no spark
Of goodness you can ne'er remark
But five or six rude motive powers,
Obeying which they spend their hours;
And in their circle, without change,
Their tedious sameness they will range.
But in a heart, though knowing ill,
That in its depths is noble still,
There are besides a thousand ways
In which, when acted on, it strays.
It seems endow'd with one sense more
Than Nature gave us from her store.
Its feelings, and its thoughts as well,
Are what the Muse alone can tell;
Although it then can suffer most,
Of real joys it still can boast;
Like Dante, passage it can find,
From hell to Paradise in mind.
So e'en dramatic interest flows
From goodness, which will interpose
Between a sad and vicious course,
When hope throughout finds no resource.

But here this great charm, soon or late,
Will lead us back to Eden's gate,
Where nought monotonous is found
On the bright, varied, spangled ground.
Then Heav'n surrounding us will lie,
As if we soar'd beyond the sky.

Now mark, for Goodness to be found
On earth we need but look around—
Where man, in God's own image framed,
Still walks, however tainted, maim'd;
So that, in fact, our Maker we
Can in our fellow-creatures see,
Apart from what defiled our race,
And spoil'd its glorious primal face.
" What charming things!" Lamartine cries,
" What hidden treasures to surprise,
In human nature do we find,
So simple, loving, brave, and kind!
Oh, who could fathom the abyss
Of sensibility, or miss
Beholding the variety
So free from notoriety,
Called forth from novel situations,
Of fond affection indications,
The secret piety, and love
For what is the whole earth above?
The sense, and the poetic feeling,
Which every hour seems revealing!

Yes, when the inward fact one sifts,
What prodigality of gifts!
In man's frail nature what a grace,
What genius in our common race!"
The joys that flow from common things,
No Poet from Parnassus sings.
Yet if uncommon, each would seem
The rapture of a fairy dream.
Take only woman, still as made
To cheer man in the happy shade
From which, alas! both wander'd, till
The second Eve fulfill'd God's will;
Since which bright, glad and glorious day
Back to it led, though late their way—
In soft ethereal warmth now shown
To be the road that both will own;
In her his just fame to abide,
In him her goodness to reside.
By her, th' Italian Poet sings,
Man, to reach Heav'n, now gaineth wings;
Imparadised within her arms,
Shelter'd from pride, and all his harms;
Or she's the ladder for his feet,
Till up on high they both can meet,
When with their minds and every sense
They reap with bliss pure Innocence.
In what do women not excel?
Old Euphues could never tell.
" In love and loyalty," saith he,
" And fervour none can like them be;

And men, admitting what I state,
Will wonder more than imitate.
Yea, rather will they laugh than try
To emulate, or with them vie.
But as for me," he adds, " I own
All Paradise seems open thrown,
As often as my mind surveys
Pure woman's virtues, woman's ways.
In Heav'n itself was recognized
That grace which is on earth so prized—
The maid, soft, modest, pensive, fair,
Seen as an angel every where.
'Twas goodness of the woman's mind,
In part, which saved the human kind.
Without that gentle Hebrew maid,
Our debts, as now, had not been paid;
Since, after all, 'twas her reply,
Accordant with the secret high,
Which was requirëd for our race
By Him who would the sins efface
Of the whole world; so well may we
In her find true felicity,
And blazon'd 'midst the altar's light
See those who can our hearts delight,
To whom, in one sense, thus we owe
Both Heav'n above and Heav'n below.
Descend we from such radiance full,
And think but of the beautiful—
Of the enchantment woman throws
O'er all the scenes through which she goes,

So long as brave she will resist
Those who on changing her insist,
And still a woman will remain,
However sophists may complain
Like him who said, " You seem to me
Nothing that's wise to know, or be."
Though she may scorn old Solon's law,
And after her whole shoploads draw,
Instead of only dresses three,
And boxes suitable, to be
One cubit high, and nothing more,
It matter'd not who might implore—
The utmost that he would permit
To her, the quantum he deem'd fit—
I say, if disregarding this,
There must be piles to follow miss—
Baskets and trunks, both high and strong
Which all unto herself belong;
Yet still you can't but love her whim,
When she defies, and laughs at him.
And after all, as we know well,
None now command a Fairy's spell,
As when the Princess, with Perrault,
Would from the stately Palace go,
And Lilas bade her take no care,
For all her toilette should be where
She might arrive, and wish to change
The ass's skin, that costume strange.
Yes, follow her, the Fairy said,
Should all, wherever she was sped.

Her gowns and jewels, under ground
Whenever wanted should be found.
There are no Fairies in our day,
So travel thus girls never may.
There must be noise, and toil, and fuss;
At least, what's visible to us
Above ground, or as now e'en under,
Still seen by men, to make them wonder.
But, whether you agree with me
Or not, one truth at least you'll see,—
That wheresoe'er we turn we find
The graces of the female mind,
The thoughts peculiar to the sex,
E'en when they startle and perplex.
It gives our spirit lightsome wings
To hear a woman's view of things—
The sweet variety to trace
Which English madmen would efface,
Just as if they themselves became
Like women on whom Greece cried "Shame!"
Whom Aristophanes has shown,
Met and resolved no peers to own,
Each social custom to review,
To change, and there make all things new,
That so emancipated, free,
They might become, for all to see—
Like men, though what was meant will seem
To us a hideous, loathsome dream.
Whereas, the wisest love to find
The woman with a female mind,

The contrasts playful which arise
From seeing life with her arch eyes;
Which now, if all were train'd alike,
Would no more thus our fancy strike.
Melampus, Amythaon's son,
Pausanias says great fame had won,
When Argien women were thought mad,
And he some wondrous secret had,
To cure them of their frantic vein
In Anaxagoras's reign.
In houses none of them could rest;
To run through fields they thought was best.
But run about they might for me,
Nor madness would that seem to be.
Some sophist, doubtless, was the Leech,
Who would immure them all, and each;
Though I admit that homes and towns
From them receive their brightest crowns,
So that from women still should be
Their names to all posterity;
As from their women aye were named
The cities of Beotia famed—
Platea, and still many more,
Immortalized in Grecian lore;
Though Cleodore, the Nymph's hard lot,
Is to be now almost forgot;
While her own son, Parnassus, still
Gives title to that glorious hill.
But roam, or rest, or run, or sit,
Nought is so joyous as their wit.

Whate'er you call them from their haunts,
They have their magic, without vaunts;
Whether Oreades they be,
Aye wandering o'er the mountains free,
Or Dryads, forests deep among;
Or Hamodryads, from trees sprung;
Or Naïds, whom the fountains lave;
Or Nereids of the ocean wave.
It is their frolic, and their play,
Which drives from us all gloom away.
Woman life's choicest prize has won,
She spreads more brightness than the sun.
At one sly word from her sweet lips,
'Tis nameless pleasure that man sips.
What 'tis there's none on earth can tell;
We only know 'tis what is well.
On her 'tis thus oft Heav'n descends
As gaily through the crowd she wends—
Pure womanhood, in which it lies
To see all things without surprise.
To her belongs that sweet content
Which ne'er to murmuring is bent,
That insight into all our hearts,
Expecting us to play our parts
Of boy or man; alike resign'd
To bear with each thing in its kind;
She seldom thinks it might be better,
She takes us even to the letter.
She'll laugh, perhaps, but then she'll say,
That after all it is our way;

As if, whatever nature wills,
Her wish, all innocence, fulfils.
The common rule, the common sense,
She never thinks can need defence.
Decorum and propriety
Are what she ever likes to see:
For in her mind she'll never hold,
To fashion each, a special mould,
Some fabrication of her brain;
For all such schemes she thinks are vain.
With knowledge of small humble things,
Which her peculiar instinct brings.
With observations wide, acute,
Of what each age and rank will suit,
She takes for granted all our ways
Are what some law supernal sways.
To her one family appears
All London, which she so endears,
As if, submissive, still it went
With movements like the firmament.
But when the love of order thus
Directs, without parade or fuss,
Where no eccentric notions jar,
Sweet Heav'n from minds cannot be far;
Since, after all, the social state
Is what Heav'n's wisdom does create.
Grave Cato was not happy, as they say,
Regarding women, and with them his way.
Might it not be, as Plutarch humbly asks,
That he their patience often overtasks?

That cold, harsh manners push'd to an extreme,
However wise, to them repulsive seem?
Untemper'd by the gentleness of Phocion,
Of Cato's sense they might not have a notion.
That he their hearts should alienate from him,
Yields no great proof of their distemper'd whim;
As still may be observed without surprise,
Where proud, vain gravity with Cato vies.
But what avails the sophist's deep disdain,
When all his crew will of the sex complain?
The light of Heav'n will no less shine around,
Though owls are blind, and bats see nothing
    found.

Goodness, quite free from all convention's strife,
From all the purse-proud vanities of life—
Goodness express'd in some sweet maiden's face,
Yes, daily, here in London you can trace,
Mark'd in each gesture, in the soft, kind smile,
Controll'd by graces that would ne'er beguile,
Seen at a moment's glance in manners dear,
That make you feel as if some angel near.
No pride of station, only nature there—
Nought upon earth so lovely and so fair!
'Tis Heav'n descends, if they should chance to stay,
And Heav'n remains when they have pass'd away;
For goodness leaves a memory behind,
That bathes in sweetness the enchanted mind;
And while the soul possessing it is blest,
Who but perceive it find themselves at rest—

Yea, in the lap of sweet contentment laid,
As if good they themselves were likewise made;
No word exchanged, yet solitary not,
As though the fact of stranger were forgot;
No more with inward struggles left alone,
But all another's goodness now their own,
Until the changing pageantry of time
Has chased the visions of another clime.

Then take but Home, with other joys,
An image oft the Bard employs.
Oh, the sweet air of natal ground
When woman such a guide is found!
Like my enskied, seraphic Jane
While here on earth she would remain!
That love of our own native land,
Our homestead with its looks so bland!
Oh, what can equal that great treasure,
So near to true celestial pleasure?
Which springs from being Home the true,
An image of which here we view.
Ah, like Sertorius, we should be
Preferring its humility,
Though poverty be with us there,
To riches in a foreign air;
Our native field, our native town,
To thrones elsewhere that yield a crown.
Then, where a dwelling can you find,
That has not some wise Uraque kind?

Like that good soul of whom we read,
As ready to assist each need,—
Melior's sister would none vex,
As found with Blois' Partenopex.
And what if rules at home should be
From women's influence not free,
What if the household only prove
The power and extent of love—
The power, therefore, of that dress,
Which men by homely terms express,
Is that a reason we should fear
Lest perfect bliss cannot be here?
A famous spirit will supply
An instance, taken from the sky.
Saith he, just now there sprung a lark,
Whose flight and song I did remark.
Up from the ground he gaily rose;
The morning light around him glows,
As if he would salute the sun;
But scarcely was his song begun,
When from the self-same spot of ground
His lady love to rise did bound;
Close to him flew that pretty dear,
But what she said I could not hear,
Though I inferred she had found fault
With somewhat, as no doubt she ought;
For down upon the ground again
She flew, and he then ceased his strain;
Just took a slight twirl in the air,
And follow'd her, to nestle there.

The whole affair was simply this:
An instance of domestic bliss.
All animated nature so
The paths to happiness can show.

Each house, by animals alone,
Entwined about each heart seems grown,
As when the Tyrrhidæan boys
Reap'd from their stag domestic joys,
That creature loving their soft hand,
Train'd to its master's table bland,
Still wand'ring through the woods by day,
Homewards each eve to take its way
To the known bounds, the home for all,
Where each so loves sweet nature's call.
The horse or pony e'en can yield
To youth a true Elysian field.
The dog or cat too both are sent
To us with the same kind intent.
Why dost thou now such names disdain,
As suiting not a poet's strain?
The pleasure yielded by them all,
At least to children, is not small;
And childhood, as our Lamb has said,
Is not yet from the world so fled,
That its great joys grave wits should find
Unworthy the eternal mind.
So animals domestic thus
Are brought in playing here by us;

Not like the dog and cat of Titien,
Misplaced, an infamous addition
To that grand, deep, impressive scene
Where our great risen Lord is seen.
Their frolics there do but disgust!
Here, own them rightly placed we must.
No, all these little common things,
When thus observed, to thoughts give wings;
Nor do I dread here to repeat,
That for all mankind they are sweet,
Again, not willing to discard
The tame creatures of each farm-yard.
O Elia, how your song is sweet,
Enraptured with each thing you meet!
I love that wizard when he stops
To praise the sight and sound of shops,
And of each item in the street
That smiling can his fond eyes meet—
Endow'd with that old English fun
Which can immortalize a pun,
And render precious to our eye
Whate'er he once saw passing by.
Catch but his spirit, and you'll throw
A charm on daily life's least show,
Which, preternaturally seen,
Will only yield to Heav'n's own sheen.
Mere common objects then will rise
To starry heights 'fore mental eyes:
"The Seven Sisters," Annie, then
Will be new Pleiads for such men;

The road call'd from them where you stray
Will shine another milky way;
Street children on their errands sent
Will mount into the firmament;
Constellatory light will rest
On faces, and each act invest;
Admiring all things, you will stand
Enchanted, as in Eden's land,
Like man primæval, wond'ring still,
While sun and stars their course fulfil.

To such a mind the world presents a view
Where all things seem to wear an aspect new,
Creatures, not spirits, constantly in sight,
Little inferior to Heaven's spirits bright,
As if a daily intercourse you find,
'Twixt the angelic and the human mind,
As if in just gradation all were framed
That no one by harsh contrasts should be shamed,
Plebeian angels, popular in show
Yielding to none while waiting on the low.
Then patriarchs break stones upon the road,
And cherubs hover o'er the poor abode;
O Lumley, now to me be ever near,
And all this transformation will appear!
The boy that whistles, or so gaily sings,
Seems clad with azure, wearing golden wings;
Aged holy saints sell apples in the street;
And youths that buy have plumes that reach their feet;

The sons of labour fill your soul with shame,
To think that you in worth are not the same;
The groups of children, as by Raphael's hand
Look down through clouds, or rapt in glory stand;
The lads that toil, or have such honest glee,
Transport you to the roof of Galilee;
And that is to unfold not Heav'n alone;
But the great Lord of all whom seraphs own.
The crowds, when pulses beat as in one breast
Impart the union of th' eternal rest;
A halo shines around the maiden's face;
And Heav'n's own denizens in all you trace;
The change is not mere fanciful, but true—
Deny it, and the fault will be in you;
To have dispeopled Heav'n, some may boast,
But here on earth they are mistaken most;
So seldom are your positivists right,
When even judging what is in their sight;
The goodness may seem dormant in the heart
But there it lies prepared to play its part,
At least, like that of Pericles, whose boast
In ancient times denoted goodness most—
That no Athenian in his mind, or limb,
Had ever felt a pain produced by him.

'Tis true, I know, the good do oft complain
Of strange wild fancies flitting through their brain,
Suggested by the thousand things they meet,
Which prove not only strange, but also sweet,

Removed the farthest from whate'er is haughty,
Perhaps relations distant of the naughty,
Wearing no cloak to argue the precise,
But rather feeling they're not over nice.
There are who of such fancies have a host
But never of their secret flights to boast,
When they will take an airing thus beyond
The diocese of strictness, feeling fond
Of green recesses where no hunter fierce,
Can follow them through those wild shades to pierce.
Thus eyes are fix'd to see a roadster stand
Awaiting wanton and a stern command,
And pleased, perhaps, whenever they can see
A certain new and vulgar chivalry.
These link'd associations will abide
Wherever can be found a harmless side.
Things most ridiculous when found alone,
Acquire thus oft a secret pleasant tone.
For Nature prompts to watch, and touch, and scent
That which from pleasing, nothing can prevent.
Sensational emotion thus will play
A private part e'en in a well-spent day,
Not needing actions hurtful and insane
As in the fictions now that are so vain,
Hurtful to ourselves, as well to others,
Which conscience never justifies and covers,
But simple aquiescence in some voice
Of Nature, leaving high and low no choice,
But that of yielding to the harmless call
To feel in secret and to relish all;

Enjoying Nature as she ebbs and flows
Through wild impressions that each mortal knows,
Which ne'er are hinted at in free discourse,
Though not in secret recognized as coarse,
But rather, as to innocence allied,
E'en having an engaging homely side.
So people who with good aye most agree,
Will sometimes ride off on a mental spree,
Will feel inclined harsh thoughts of blame to scout,
While e'en "their mothers know not they are out;"
If you'll forgive the Muse for flying low,
As if our London mirth she too can know;
But like a bird, she will pick up in streets
Some idle fancy that her purpose meets;
As when she would now indicate the train
Of those sensations, which she knows are vain.
Goodness is frank, and never will allow
Her real friends these thoughts to disavow.
Sooth, rational these are not, as we know;
But that prevents not sympathy to flow.
Proclaim them with assurance no one must,
Though only tainted with our parent dust.
And yet, who knows? perhaps it may be said
They have to purer things than this earth led.
Unbridle passion; and the mind grows cool,
'Tis heated most when subjected to rule;
Just as a horse whose temper is the best,
When spurr'd and held in, never is at rest.
Besides, perhaps, where goodness is unknown,
The same impressions minds will seldom own.

Men most opposed to goodness never know
Why any being should be tempted so.
Analyze these feelings if you dare,
A certain homely tenderness is there.
They spring from deep affection for our race
Which humblest ways of love would still embrace;
Ways e'en enjoin'd as antidotes to pride,
Which prudery to Nature has denied.
What pride would deem absurd humiliation
These would accept with secret admiration,
As yielding even an artistic sense
Of Beauty, which the cold world chases hence,
A secret wish to realize the text
With no such great remorse need be purplex'd.
And those who would no human being harm,
Can still find shelter 'neath an angel's arm;
The sun still shines on matter, as of yore,
While spirit sees it, and will higher soar.
The mind gives purity quite of its own
To fancies—to reality unknown;
And e'en reality directed thus
Grows mentally all purified for us.
Kind Heav'n, we think, will look with other eyes
On him who proudly sees, and all defies.
A holy Virgin even, we are told
By Heisterbach, so wise with legends old,
Preferr'd what the grave Muse declines to name
To crimes of Spirit, which we seldom blame.
Said she, "The first is simply human still;
The last denotes a diabolic will."

Stern harshness for one's self, as well as others,
Is what this daily observation smothers;
And that removed, the passage is more free
To reap on earth sweet Heav'n's felicity,
Which reigns not always in high thoughts sublime,
But grants a rapture from our mortal slime.
And after all there may be some excess,
When seeking such impressions to suppress.
To this thought Michael Angelo was led,
Who, sculpture new and old comparing, said,
" We take away too much of matter now;
When all, unlike the Greeks, we don't allow
The form to show itself combined with thought,
Instead of both respecting, as we ought.
So forms too pale, diaphanous we make,
And this, too, for the pure idea's sake.
Too much importance we ascribe to one,
Until we find the other fled, and gone;
Although we own is due pre-eminence
To mind o'er all that's subject to the sense."
The Muse at least would wish us to unlearn
What represented Goodness cold and stern.
She wings a varied flight o'er dale and hill,
And ne'er suspects all pleasure to be ill.
She thinks that oft impressions may arise,
Which are forgiven where the mischief dies.
That as the mists of earth grow colour'd bright,
Presenting rainbows to the charm'd sight;
So vapours, springing from our human mould,
Can change to pledges of a love untold.

But onwards let us now pursue
This path, and other objects view.

Past doubt, there is a class below
Of men who do not clearly show
That they would hence to Eden stray,
Or even ask to learn the way.
Alien from Heav'n, their looks alone
Suffice to tell from whence they're flown.
No love, though each may be a " brother,"
Either to God or to each other.
In Italy, or Spain, or France,
You can detect them at a glance;
In England, as in Germany,
Their figures still more gross can be.
At the first glimpse your spirits sink,
As if you would dull Lethe drink;
Although you know not what they are,
You know from Heav'n must be far
The souls that on the face have left
Proof that of good they are bereft.
For once you'd say that Locke was right,
That Matter thinks, in Nature's spite;
But thinks as far as self alone,
With no more spirit than a stone,
That would ensconce itself in dross,
With clay its substance to emboss.
Such figures, met with every day,
Yield no great bliss to charm our way,

Nor guide us to the happy groves
Through which, as Paradise, one roves—
Unless that contrasts indicate
Who have or have not pass'd the gate.
Then there are gloomy faces found
That willingly would seek the ground,
If strange, dark malice did not try
To scowl on those who pass them by,
With prying looks to pierce them through,
As if they would their faults review.
In their sinistrous, dark, round face,
I grant, no gleams of Heav'n you trace.
It is suspicion that you see,
With wrath that scarce seeks secrecy.
Before that evil eye will fall
The hearts it scares and does appal.
The lovers who remark their frown
Find all their spirits sinking down.
The libertine will think himself,
Compared with such, an honest elf.
The just and holy man, and pure,
Detesting all such looks demure,
Will grieve, and inwardly complain,
That earth alone is here again.
Religion veils her face with shame,
And dreads to hear her sacred name
Associated with a sight
That turns her day to murky night;
She sees her foe conceal'd and arm'd
With all that souls have ever harm'd—

The Pharisee who knows the law,
Who charity will never draw
From all his studies of the text
With which he has the truth perplex'd;
While observation simply cries,
Such contrasts wing us for the skies.
Though some stray sheep will wander on,
Until for ever they are gone;
Whose fatal course must be ascribed
To those whom we have just described,
Who scare away and cause disgust
By threats and sentences unjust.
Seen of themselves, these sights I own,
Have Eden's entrances ne'er shown;
But then, the while e'en as they pass
You see some fair angelic lass,
Some boy or aged man, or the poor,
All bound for sweet Heav'n you are sure;
At whose bright smiles the earthly way
Grows lighter than the noon-tide day;
For when in fellowship with these,
'Tis fields Elysian that one sees.
Ah! goodness is more widely sown
Than moralists are found to own.
Observe, and then you'll quickly find
The graces of the human mind.
The faults of many even spring
From some right fair and beauteous thing!
If you will only search below,
And learn what fruits were meant to grow.

Angelic goodness you might find,
If you to goodness were not blind.
E'en Poets poor Narcissus blamed,
And saw self-love when he was named;
But that Beotian fountain clear
To him show'd her who was so dear;
Whom he resembled, so that he
Thought it was her that he did see,
When in it he beheld his face,
And her sought fondly to embrace.
'Twas love for her that made him fly,
And not self-love that made him die,
As Moralists, distorting truth,
Calumniated generous youth.

Then look at labour's varied field,
And mark what pleasures it can yield;
While honest industry supplies
That with which grandeur seldom vies;
Though losing honesty, no more
Can e'er be lost from man's whole store.
Arnigio's Vigils make you see
How every trade can Eden be.
He follows each line through details;
And lifting, as it were, the veils
Which screen from view its blissful groves,
He shows how man through pleasure roves.
But, mark, from goodness all this springs,
From seeing the bright side of things,

Which meaneth only that we find
Bright Heav'n thrown open in the mind,
Not only in the cloister cell,
But where the common people dwell.
See first that sweet Nymph, Duty call'd,
By no dread hardships e'er appall'd—
No, nor by death itself we know,
As all experience still can show;
And the Megæra's engineer
Alone will make that fact appear.
See with her, walking hand-in-hand,
Obedience free, while ever bland;
And when you daily mark the twain,
You witness bright Heav'n here again;
For Duty and Obedience still
Wait there upon the sovereign will.
Necessitude they always know,
But sheer necessity not so;
For some distinctions, though spun fine,
While right or wrong, I'd use as mine;
And old grammarians thus explain
The difference between the twain:
Necessitude hears Duty's call;
Necessity is lord of all,
Base cowards heeding only force,
Against which they find no resource.
Then even in the worst of states,
In spite of impious debates,
In spite of despots, mobs, decrees,
'Tis freedom personal one sees,

For sophists even ne'er can bind
The dulcet liberty of mind—
That freedom, gift of God on high,
Which man to man would oft deny—
Not what a tribune did invoke,
When once to rise he would provoke
The Romans to resist the law,
Against their Ædiles swords to draw,
" What skills it crying to be free,
If we can't die through luxury?
Can't perish in it even so,
The only Liberty we'd know?"
But that grand Freedom which is found
Reaching to true Elysian ground,
Where all angelic life is free,
Which we approach by liberty,
The true, that knows a just restraint
Which vile ambition cannot taint.

But as through these sweet fields we stray,
We find more spirits on our way
That open to us paths above
Whatever most on earth we love.
For what as "liberal" we praise,
Distinguishes these earthly ways,
Grown truly spacious every side,
Which reach to Heav'n's own meadows wide.
All narrow, selfish, cruel bounds
Once levell'd, near are Eden's grounds.

And so 'tis here within the mind
Disinterested, capacious, kind;
Though not obnoxious any more
To Solon's law in days of yore,
Prescribing, when it grew too wide,
That men should always take a side,
And not, through love of selfish ease,
Seek good and bad alike to please—
Nor yet deserving the reproof
Of Theopompus, who aloof
Would stand from one who boasted ever
Himself from home-ties aye to sever,
From loving foreigners aye named,
In his own country therefore blamed—
" My friend, 'twere better far if you
Your countrymen still ever knew
As one who loved his own land best,
Howe'er he might esteem the rest.
For ' Philopolites ' should be,
Not ' Philolacon ' used for thee."
A mind, as liberal as air,
For all such limits might be there.
What some call " liberal" is now
A mask for what they won't avow.
The end of all their vaunted claim
Is to recur to what they blame,
Ascribing views to those they hate,
That them they need not tolerate.
But men call'd liberal, with truth
Are Nature's darlings in their youth;

Though club-house sages they may shock,
By standing on a mental rock.

Oh, hail thou spirit, noble, pure,
Past earth, time, death, that will endure,
Now call'd by a new term oft shamed,
While thou ought'st never to be blamed.
I hail already thy sweet light
Which can restore to men their sight,
That they may equity behold,
And not be to a party sold,
By the side, generous to be
Of every party they can see;
But by their evil side of none,
Though left in solitude alone;
For sharpest eyes with films are blind
When men to others are not kind—
Kind to make due allowance still
For a poor, weak, erroneous will;
Still kind to make all others free,
And awed by despots ne'er to be,
Stern despots on a little scale,
But whose deep malice might prevail
In leaving homeless, desolate
The poor who lived before their gate—
Yes, kind, to substitute themselves,
And then to judge of fragile elves,
Aye, kind, to make their goodness shine
On all, and so become divine.

And then, at least, in realms of mind,
What lasts the longest you will find
To be the ways and deeds of those
Who are to all injustice foes.
King Theopompus was disdain'd
By his own wife, who much complain'd,
That to his children he would leave
Less than when it he did receive
The regal power, when he replied,
"Nay, greater, and on every side;
Because more lasting it will prove,
As resting on a country's love."

Still onwards to felicity;
And, lo! fair Generosity!
Ah, what a sweet and gracious maid
That ushers to Elysian shade!
The generous are angels here,
Already wing'd they all appear,
Like Abdiel, the seraph full
Of zeal, the true and beautiful;
For, oh, with what celestial speed
Fly they to help another's need!
You think 'tis earth they see around?
In Heav'n they are already found.

Ah, truly sweet might be a minstrel's song
Who would describe the manners that belong

To him whom generosity inspires,
Whose portrait each beholder loves, admires!
His heart no envy knows,
No envy in it grows;
Of a tongue well skill'd to blame,
He will ever fly the shame;
And, use what speech he will,
The Muse would praise him still;
His privilege is great,
As thus she will relate;
He only can love money, and be free
From avarice, a moral prodigy;
He only can betray a wish to save,
And yet be known as one who always gave.
Oh, never, never would he, I aver,
Like Brutus, great and grave philosopher,
Have stoically his piled money lent
At interest only forty-eight per cent.,
As we can now learn from Cicero,
In his epistles that you so well know.
But then, I grant, this gay wight is not wise,
Like famous patriots of classic guise,
Each, doubtless, a true stern Republican,
While he, poor swell, is but an honest man,
Recalling that old writer's style profound,
When thus he will his model type propound.
" We well may wish to see that happy man
Whom Aristotle paints; we never can.
In vain we'd seek the orator to find
Whom Tully draws.   We see him but in mind.

Whereas, my youthful imp, though every way
Most perfect, you see daily, and can say,
He yet is common—a mere common wight—
Who every day and hour may come in sight "—
Not generous alone, his will to trust,
But, to be like all others, simply just.
To charity he dares not make pretension,
And of his secret acts if there be mention,
The grave and formal shake their heads and say
Pronounce upon them now they never may,
Unless they know the whole concatenation
Of circumstances, and the parties' station.
" It may be all quite right," say they, " or wrong;
To sift each case they fear would keep them long."
For these poor fellows often dare not tell
To whom they give, or could they name them well.
Perhaps they're sometimes by soft beauty sway'd;
Is that a reason we should them upbraid?
Perhaps misfortunes of the young and fair
May grieve them more than sorrow seen elsewhere.
They're no less found, though human, if you will,
Congenial with what's highest, purest, still.
And their deep motives, blamed by men call'd sage,
Are drawn in secret from the Gospel's page;
To visit little friends they think decorum,
And most, *in tribulatione nunc eorum.*
The common mortal will abandon those
Whose weakness the redoubted public knows;
But this is to be weaker even still
Than them, and to betray a deeper ill.

The generous the weakest will protect,
And most when no return they can expect;
They dare such resolutions firm to own;
But this belongs to greatest souls alone.
The weak are sure to disavow each other,
They fly at once like hunted game to cover.
The generous will never sacrifice
The weak to any end where interest lies [1].
Their faults, God help them! they perhaps well know;
But that prevents not tenderness to flow.
They think if they themselves were stricken down,
They would not like to see an old friend frown.
Suppose that some who press them may deceive;
Still what of that? their mother too was Eve.
And then old Honour's voice they love to hear,
And think obeying it dispels all fear.
In his kind acts employing honour still,
As cause efficient of his constant will,
Each will prove faithful to his lightest word,
When strict compliance would be deem'd absurd,
By what is styled " the public, sage, opinion,"
When sentiment makes part of its dominion.
He might, with its applause, a victim brave;
Of his own word once whisper'd he's the slave.
In brief, these men dare not submit their books
To one who imperfection never brooks.
They humbly kneel in churches next the door;
They sometimes dread e'en mercy to implore;

[1] Vauvenargues.

Samaritans and sinners seem to them
To wear a robe of which they'd touch the hem.
Some slight bright words of Heav'n's own grace they mark,
Which turns to glorious radiance what was dark;
They bring the precious ointment and the love;
The rest is only known to God above.
And yet, sweet Mantuan soul, long since to thee
It seem'd half known, when thou in mind didst see,
'Midst priests of holy ways while life did last,
And prophets who the future could forecast,
And those who spoke things worthy of the lyre
Of great Apollo who did them inspire,
And those who polish'd life by varied art
To sweeten manners and uplift the heart—
When amidst such thou sawest those who needs
Of others satisfied by gracious deeds,
" Help'd them through sorrows with benignity,
And made them cherish, love their memory,"
These thou didst place, in thy immortal song,
With the great, happy tribes who pass'd along.
The generous, thou singest, likewise wore
That snowy wreath which never fadeth more.

But open the Romance call'd of the Rose,
Which figures in accordance doth disclose,
In manuscript of the fine fourteenth age,
With gracious paintings placed between each page

"Largesse," or Generosity, you see—
A slender maiden smiling graciously,
With one arm slightly stretch'd, as to advise,
And goodness beaming from her youthful eyes—
The whole with such a kind and playful air,
You only wish you could yourself be there
To hear the gentle words that sweetly flow
To guide, while bounty large she will bestow;
The little preacher acts so well her part
Of counsellor, she steals away your heart.

Well, back we turn to tread the plainest way,
Though in these hopes we seem'd not far astray.
Ah, there were times when men seem'd more inclin'd
To honour thoughts and actions of this kind.
By a grim law the later Romans kept,
'Twas death to come near where their Ruler slept.
Aurelian, hearing from his bed a cry,
When for this cause a Greek was led to die,
Ask'd if 'twas for himself he came to plead,
As then to interfere there was no need;
"But if," said he, "it was to pray for others,
Let him go free; all guilt that object covers."
Antonio de Guevara cites the same,
Whose "golden letters" well deserve their name,
When teaching thus his Andalusian friend
That joys of generosity ne'er end :—
" 'Tis our Castilian honour, so to say,"
He adds, "that we should give, still give away ;

Yea, even till we necessaries want—
Then great indeed the glory we can vaunt!
Or, rather, sweet the secret joys we find
On earth, become a Paradise for mind."

But visions now on visions come,
Transporting to Elysium some.
For Pity steals forth, looking shy,
Encompass'd with Divinity;
She follows paths both dark and cold,
But see! oh, what do you behold?
The lost and the forlorn now smile;
Their grief she knows how to beguile.
And those whom she had weeping found,
She leaves e'en laughing in a round.
She has her tear, her gift, her mirth;
And then no more she sees the earth.
Heav'n's radiance plays around her head;
Though no one speak; it all is said.
Nor think that she is e'en confined
To human beings in her mind.
The class uncultivated kill
For sport all creatures—such their will.
They buy, entrap, then shoot by rules,
And call those who condemn them, fools.
I style the " class uncultivated "
Those who with princes may be rated,
If their light hearts be changed to stone
When they should hear " the creatures " moan;

And though, with flashy knowledge fed,
They may possess a well-cramm'd head,
Have seen the globe from pole to pole,
And thought that they must know the whole.
Soft, gentle feelings seldom flow
Through minds that only seek to know,
Which thoughts Divine have never nourish'd,
While skill and cleverness have flourish'd.
If strangers to those thoughts they be,
They take delight in cruelty—
Merely from letting be effaced
All that sweet Nature there had traced,
And leaving there an odious blank;
In them soft Pity never sank.
But she is of poetic mould;
For birds her bosom ne'er is cold;
For brutes she has no less a heart;
And she will always take their part.
But, unlike those who men exclude
From love, as does the silly prude
Who fondles cats and "pretty Polly,"
As if all other alms were folly;
She thinks the most of human woes,
As soon each man and woman knows.
But who am I to paint her such?
Let Massillon apply his touch;
For who, I ask, oh, who but he,
Can show her great felicity?
As he presents her to his king,
Then young, and does conviction bring,

That all life's other pleasures leave
Empty the cup that does deceive;
While this soft maiden, beautiful.
Keeps your vast heart for ever full;
Since aye she representeth Him
Who makes it overflow the brim.
" To thee," saith he, " I do appeal;
Say what doth grandeur make thee feel?
Then, not awaiting thy reply,
Behold how pain from thee can fly.
Employ thy wealth for this great end,
The miserable to befriend—
Each day to make less wretched those
Who probably are steep'd in woes,
Like Job, who wish their day of birth
Had seen them cover'd in the earth.
Oh, then thou'lt find thy heart dilate,
And glad that thou thus wert born great.
Be that the privilege you court;
To that be ever your resort.
The rest is all for others shown;
This, and this only, is your own.
The rest proves bitter to the taste,
While this will sweeten all in haste;
For doing good rejoices more
Than your receiving it with store.
Return to it then day by day,
'Tis joy that never fades away.
The oftener you taste it so,
More worthy of it you will grow.

Custom can deaden other joys;
Your own prosperity but cloys;
But prosperous to make another,
Proves joy that habit will not smother.
Each act of kindness with it brings
A secret bliss that hath no stings;
And custom which can harden hearts
Gainst other joys, to this imparts
A freshness and a novel pleasure,
As if each time you found a treasure
Before that moment never known,
And that new wealth is made your own."
But how could it be otherwise?
Or why should any feel surprise,
Since the soft path you pass along
To Heav'n's great Lord does all belong?
It is through Paradise you stray;
The gloom of earth has pass'd away;
Around you the bright angels singing,
And your own joyous heart still winging,
As if no more on earth you trod,
But, soaring high, conversed with God.
Ah! passing thus beyond the bounds
Of earth, you will not hear the sounds
Of the Virgilian voice, that cried
To him who Tartarus defied,
" Why seek by toil that is insane,
To feed your mind with what is vain?"
But here myself I must defend
From critics, who will scorn expend.

To play the orator, they cry,
Is not the part of poetry;
And great Quintillian did complain
Of Lucan singing such a strain.
It may be so; but yet his name
Is not less known by endless fame;
And what are the Pharsalian fields,
To the choice sweets that goodness yields?
So we who cull from every flower
May no less haunt the Muse's bower.

But now the view will change, when we
Still other graces come to see.
For suddenly the thunder rolls,
And Justice opes her solemn scrolls;
For Justice too must claim her dole
On earth, and steel the human soul.
No wrath like ours, no passion there—
But righteousness that will compare
Deeds, and then simply, nobly act
In strict accordance with each fact;
As Bossuet did ears astound,
By saying that "a man was found,"
And adding no reproaches loud
While comprehended by the crowd,
Hearing in History's solemn voice
That justice which doth all rejoice.
For Neoptolemus is then
A symbol to admonish men,

Whose punishment it was to suffer
What he inflicted on another.
He Priam at the altar slew,
And later was himself in view
Slain at Apollo's altar, where
To Delphi suppliants repair.
Then men, inspirëd by this sense,
In their own cause urge no pretence,
But place themselves within the scale
Where that maid's sentence must prevail.
The statesman who is just for all
Finds Heaven descending at his call.
For when a Gladstone braves a throng,
To right a people—cancel wrong—
Moments there are in his career
When bliss unearthly must be near.
But when he is the same as now,
Who mercy no less will avow,
Who opens wide the prison door
That captives there may pine no more,
Who boldly will disdain the cry
Of those ne'er touch'd by misery—
Disdain to calculate if men
Will prove themselves as grateful then,
Or, owning spirits of the day,
Pretend they have no thanks to pay,
Who, heeding Justice above all,
Attends no less to Pity's call,
And bids the wretched to be free,
Once more the fields and hills to see—

Obnoxious to the sneers of those
Who Charilaus did oppose,
As being but a soft, good man,
Without a will, or any plan
To punish, finding in his heart
No strength to play another part.
Him let false politicians blame,
But poets aye will bless his name;
Though what is praise from human lips
To him who Heaven's Ambrosia sips?
For him the raptures of the sky,
With Heav'n on earth that instant nigh;
For rulers wielding power so
Have joys surpassing all below.

Helvetius said that interest sway'd
All motives that the best men made.
So said the sophists, who pretend
That henceforth men should have for end
The interest of whole nations, not
Of individuals forgot,
The interest of some future races,
Which present misery effaces—
The less of pity now with crimes,
The happier all future times,
Securing thus immortal fame,
Which will the past and present shame;
They think they will obtain it more
By sending Pity from the door.

The " Interest General" was then
" An armëd doctrine" for such men—
As old as Epicurus still,
New-model it as Paley will.
Fabricius pray'd that it might be
His country's direst enemy,
Who that base maxim would receive,
His nation ruin'd so to leave.
But whate'er Pyrrhus might admire,
Or Cineas to teach desire,
The sense of Justice, not self-love,
Annexes earth to Heav'n above;
For when all selfishness thus dies,
The mind, unclogg'd, to Eden hies.
Would that men now were found to imitate
Lycurgus, abdicating royal state,
Foreseeing that perhaps a rightful heir
Might yet be born, to whom greatest care
 Was due; and, willing exile, leaving Greece,
That all suspicious fears from men might cease;
When that fair boy—then born, saluted king,
As Charilaus, peace and joy did bring
To those who wish'd his undisputed reign,
That thenceforth no one might of ill complain.
Their lives would then be happier than now,
When "facts accomplish'd" hide the broken vow.

Yes, Justice teaches us to be
From interested emotions free;

And earth is adjoin'd to Heav'n then,
When trod by such true god-like men.
E'en when to punish she is call'd,
She seems distrustful and appall'd.
For mark how she will turn aside,
Her starting tears to chase and hide!
It is that she has seen the cross,
And all man's justice changed to dross.
She flies and shows another maid,
Who spreads Elysium through the shade.
Of this poor world that now will shine
With mercy from on high divine.
At her sweet smile the darkest pit
With Heav'n's own radiance becomes lit.
Yes, in her presence, at her touch,
As this bright maid, grow even such
The hosts who aye soft mercy gave,
Who for themselves would mercy crave.
So common scenes of goodness thus
On earth ope Heaven unto us.

'Tis said a certain king did once complain
That all the world grew worse, more vile and vain.
He sent for four Philosophers to tell
Why nothing now, as formerly, was well.
The sages then repair to the four gates,
On each of which the reason each one states;
The words mysterious then were all inscribed
By which the latent evil was described.

"Power is justice, power is the law"
(I trust no future times they then foresaw)
"The day is night; and so no path is found
O'er the entangled and the darken'd ground."
"One is now two; for truth is here denied,
Through selfish interest, or from reckless pride.
Friends are but secret enemies while they
Have only fawning words to each to say.
The will is the great sole authority;
And so each home but feels calamity.
Great God is dead! and so o'er eyes of all
There hangs suspended a dark, hideous pall."
You have the tale, unmeaning now for some
Who have of late to this condition come.
No Heav'n on earth, I wot, can there be found:
May darkness such fly far from English ground,
That Eden's fields all eyes may here behold,
With Heav'n around them, as in days of old!

CANTO XII.

TO THOSE WHO HAVE BEEN LED ASTRAY.

Oh, bright is goodness merging in the goal!
But all the earth feels not its dulcet ray.
For traversary planets round us roll,
And orbits, as Astrologers display,
Of dissimilitude, as Suso said,
When men from Heav'n and joy are farther led.

You'd say the land here was a dismal plain,
O'erspread by dull, impenetrable clouds;
The senses even loudly will complain,
That all their pleasures a dull vapour shrouds.
You'd think that disappointments here must dwell,
And no faint trace be left of what is well.

For here to beauty men seem wholly blind;
You'd say no art or nature could avail
To yield one glimpse of Heav'n to the mind,
Or raise for it one instant the thick veil
Which covers what is good and fair and right,
Concealing things Divine from human sight.

It is not here, as we observed before,
That men of admiration are amerced;
It is that they dislike from their heart's core
What merits praise—all things are so reversed
That e'en to them it might be said 'tis given
"Ne'er more in Hell to be than when in Heav'n."

So to these now Creation's book is nought;
The page of genius blotted, and effaced;
High poetry and music may be brought,
But in them things of Heav'n will not be traced;
The chant of holy quires seems flat and stale,
And vainly sings for them the nightingale.

But "mysteries" there are which they can see,
As those of Paris, London, manifold,
While still for them a mere nonentity
Are Sion's wonders, which they ne'er behold.

What is the earth to them, and all its flowers,
Divested thus of their best mental powers?

They believe in nothing, do not even dream:
A hideous yawn is heard beside their couch.
The hill, the garden, field, will only seem
A disenchantment they would e'en avouch.
Morose and fruitless irony they bring,
To follow, snarling, each bright, glorious thing.

"What folly!" cry they, "are you of those men
Who think there are such things as wicked
    folk—
Imaginary beings trying then
To realize, and men of sense provoke?
This little prejudice shows vulgar taste,
Of which, for our part, we take leave in haste.

"We believe it not (disinterested the while)—
All the whole world is wicked, and is not;
Each takes and gives, and so there is no guile.
Or would you speak of words? In them, I wot,
Since there can be no merit, taste, or style
Which is not contradicted, as you see,
Since nought is true of aught, what's it to thee,

"If men say this or that on any theme?
My hero heeds it not, nor e'er should thine.
In one house wise, and in another seem
But arrant fools, the same men I opine.
When here, Erastus is a coarse buffoon,
While there, a man of wit they'll call him soon.

"If you will speak of acts, it is the same :
A well-lined purse will cover all defects :
Possessing that, no gentleman we blame ;
For nothing further any one expects.
The present age will own one only crime—
Ennui, which makes pass heavily the time.

"Amusement, business, be the twain thy care ;
The rest may fly around, and circulate ;
Breathe only what you find is in the air,
For that suits best our present social state.
Would you 'gainst modern thoughts insanely rise ?
Your ancient hoary maxims are but lies.
Let each one do and speak just what he likes ;
For all is evil, all is good together ;
This thought, as being best, our fancy strikes,
What others say will matter not a feather."
In such lines, Gresset paints the spirits here ;
Yes, just as they to us will now appear.

Love they would purchase ; God they would have sold ;
Prepared the morrow, as the past, to spurn ;
At twenty, wither'd, satiated, old,
And never knowing to what side to turn ;
Nought is for them magnificent or sweet ;
They only see the wrong that they would greet.

No, not for them will Heav'n begin on earth ;
Through glades opposed, alas ! they seem to roam
Where gnashing of the teeth, instead of mirth,
Denotes another and a bitter home ;

As if a place of woe now here begins
For " ululantes " in the toil of sins.

These, while forgetful of a better fame,
  Pursued by injured ghosts whom they have wrong'd,
Whom frigid Death has left without a name,
Reap inward darkness which to crime belong'd.
From all creation penalties they draw—
Present in every place those once they saw.

Oh, dreadful mysteries of nature here,
When Ugliness comes forth to scare the mind!
Since nothing seen can ever such appear;
And it in the invisible we find.
For the word ugliness implieth nought,
Unless in the invisible 'tis sought.

Then Asmodeus, Beemoth, Belial proud,
Abadon and Diabolus are near,
With Lucifer and Beelzebub to shroud
The bliss which could in industry appear,
Satan and Demon, Astaroth of sloth,
And Beelphegor to anger never loth,

Not now, alas! as in the ages past,
  When these were counted stript of all their might;
Since Faith still potent did with mankind last,
And deem disarmed all opposed to right.
" Poor devil!" then becoming the sole name,
For him as clothed with ridicule and shame.

But once again, with awful power clad,
Whether with Goethe, like a gentleman;
Or marked with all the symbols of the bad,
Which only hideous outlines portray can;
Insidious, artful, specious, bland to hear,
Or unmask'd, bestial, causing woe and fear.

Oh, who that sees this murky way would think
That even here are issues to the light?
Eschewing which so many spirits sink,
Embracing as their bride the vacant night;
Yet still it winds round true Elysian bowers
Ne'er closed to man while last his mortal hours.

No gate of burning adamant is there
Against us barr'd, prohibiting ingress.
Short is the way, and soft as summer's air,
That upwards leads to joy no tongues express,
To those smooth confines where the eye can trace
The gates of light, and Heav'n's own glorious face.

Yes, here, e'en here, Heav'n strangely may begin,
And Paradise celestial burst to view;
Such issues are there on the path of sin,
Of which we see the wonders old and new;
And how this great enchantment can be sought
Will soon appear, and by what means 'tis wrought.

For first 'tis happiness which man will seek;
And when he finds but misery around,
He may detect his error, although weak,
And turn his steps aside to other ground.

Then, led by motives partly low and high,
To the bright stars above the heart will fly.

Instinctively attracted to the light
Of Him, who is no eagle fierce, to soar,
No tempest, raving through the winter's night,
Nor yet a voice like lions' hideous roar;
It seeks that radiant aureole, composed
Of sweetness luminous, to wrong opposed.

A sense of solitude first 'waken'd here,
As if the soul were in a world alone,
Induces sadness not unmix'd with fear,
And makes it feel the path is not its own;
For solitary each on this must be,
However numerous the company.

Though parasites may haunt the rich each eve,
To pour their flatt'ring accents in the ear,
Though lust with fawning proffers would deceive,
And round the poor and helpless love appear,
There comes a sudden start in lonely hearts,
When blank with dread they feel what earth imparts.

Perhaps there are some spirits wholly blind
To good, mysterious in their dark abyss;
But far more often nature mix'd we find,
And e'en when lowest, capable of bliss—
Yea, e'en at moments feeling they would be
Unchain'd by custom, from its sadness free.

And then in the deformity of sin,
View'd by poor waverers 'twixt hate and fear,
A yearning for Elysium may begin,
Of which the graces will so soon appear
In household customs, memories of home,
Back to which gladness, partly thrust, they'll roam.

Far they would fly the monster that will wait
On feasts, with anger, plots and crimes to fan,
Whom Tartaræan sisters even hate,
With Pluto, as the evil only can;
A mind of vipers shedding into all;
While him by countless names we mortals call.

And, sooth, the company that take this way,
No man or woman can for aye admire;
Each may be tempted for a while to stray;
But fellowship like this at last will tire,
When bestial forms in man are shown to eyes,
And seen through is the flimsy, vain disguise.

As when of old, by the Circæan shore,
Æneas, coasting through the sable night,
Heard the wild husk-fed boars and lions roar,
With howling wolves whose cries proclaim'd their might,
Whom Circe with her herbs had changed from men,
So hear we in our streets these wild beasts' den.

In human shape the wolf, the fox is found,
The ape, the hog, the viper, and the bear,
The serpent, no more trailing on the ground,
But all erect and with a soothing air.
When sprites like these are seen beneath their mask,
To follow angels is an easy task.

Saith Heisterback, " as seeing God will prove,
Beatitude for those who are elect,
So, in beholding Satan, foe to Love,
Will be the pain of those who Him reject[1];"
And e'en on earth no punishment more great,
Than seeing those who would uphold his state.

In books Etruscan Cicero had found
Some names sinistrous which with these agree;
"*Deteriores*" and "*Repulsos*" sound
As things, he says, from which all men should flee,
From common safety far, though all they'll dare;
Of these *Deteriores*, then, beware;

"Of whom," he adds, "the nation is immense."
But now there is a nation much more vast,
With which we can be join'd without offence,
And find that common safety which will last;
It is the ancient, present, Christian fold,
Where Heav'n conjoin'd with earth we may behold.

[1] Liv. v.

Within that pale all gentleness you find,
Whate'er can cheer the heart and charm the eye,
The charities of life so gracious, kind,
The beauty which true goodness must supply.
'Tis not the dull, cold, formal, puling crew,
Which gloomy pedants would pass off for true.

Soft love, bright fancy, and great wishes pure,
Honour's high, noble, and triumphant voice,
The Hope which e'en midst failings will endure,
Bespeak that fold; and then, oh, say, what choice
Is left you when confronted with the rest,
The most pretentious, or in fact the best?

Fed on that holy mount, our feet can climb,
Aided by "God who is the same for all;"
As e'en the poet said in darkest time,
Though by false names great truths he still would
    call;
As where he added, "Fates will find a way,
Who needs must yield to th' Olympian sway."

For on that hill is Paradise regain'd—
Asylum sweet to which all faults may fly—
Where by unearthly visions minds sustain'd
Can find themselves in Heav'n before they die,
Usher'd by Mercy's hand within the bower
Where joy celestial crowns the present hour.

Each is not Lausus when he was denied
By Fortune a returning to his home,
To his own country, whence some evil pride,
Ancestral or self-taught, had made him roam.

From falls in life, or from mistakes in mind,
To the sidereal seats a way men find;

For each will sit, like great Æneas, lost
In thought, revolving many past events,
What all his struggles through his life have cost,
While baffled often were his best intents.
That mental voyage through the opaque night
Brings more than stars before his waken'd sight.

Not in reward of meritorious deed
Have they claim'd entrance to the blessed pale;
But to its flowery meadows will they speed
By knowing 'tis the cross that will avail,
And trusting in forgiveness, that is found
Of instant access to the heav'nly ground.

So taught Saint Bernard, Dante, Rupert grave,
Saint Bonaventure, Innocent the Third,
All showing with the rest the way to save
Those of the cross who have or have not heard—
D'Avila, Gertrude, she of Escobar,
Marina, each of hope a morning star.

Saint Thomas, and no less the mystic school,
Wave thus all mortals to the sacred spring,
By counsel, prayer, and sage majestic rule,
Whence to Elysian fields their way they wing,
To see bright Heav'n descending upon earth,
And join with angels in eternal mirth.

Strange mystery of Nature and of Grace,
Seeming to reign in ancient tragic song,
Where names fictitious cannot quite efface
The truth of " Remedy Divine for wrong."
As the three Acts of Æschylus can prove
The end of all is Pardon, Peace, and Love.

Name his three dramas now whate'er you will,
The same must ever be their indication;
They, all in one, embrace tradition still,
The crime, the pain, the reconciliation.
Orestes in his conscience findeth peace,
And by Apollo hath at last release.

All three are found in Life's great drama now —
The crime — whate'er that be, we must perceive,
Although, with Socrates, we should avow
Through ignorance alone men goodness leave,
The pain — ah! clear we see in those who find
E'en Nature hostile, and the world unkind.

Inseparably link'd they both are found,
The crime and pain, disclosed to every sense,
Some law eternal binds them fastly round,
Denial is but empty vain pretence.
What's left is Reconcilement of the soul,
To Peace, and Goodness, and the one great Whole.

And is this last act hidden from our eyes?
No, far more visibly it shines to us;
We see it daily, and without surprise,
Ourselves and others now forgiven thus.

CANTO XII.

Oh, let no more Apollo have the praise,
But to great God eternal eyes upraise.

This might suffice; but still a path is here
Provided for the frail who vainly stray;
The heart itself will point to it with fear,
Though wholly silent hearts, sooth, no one may;
It is the path of infinite desire,
Which oft will those most erring most inspire.

Oh, Greece! we need not cite thy magic Muse,
Though oft agreeing with our holy creed,
As when she cries, " Ah! do not all hope lose,
If good in thee should failings still exceed;
Human thou art; but well 'tis with thee then;"
For higher voices will now sound to men.

Saint Austin said, addressing God in prayer,
"Oh, if thou wert not God, thou wert unjust;
For while to sin we creatures often dare,
Thou teachest us in mercy still to trust.
Forgive," he adds, " the madness of the word
Which sounds a wild delirium, and absurd."

Saint Bernard doth relate a wondrous tale
Of one who dying could not grieve for sin,
To show that frankness is of great avail,
When greatest sinners still would mercy win.
The priest who heard him would consult the saint,
And thus his own great difficulty paint.

For, "Sir," said his weak penitent, "I grieve
That for my sins I cannot sorrow feel,
I would not pain you, nor, still less, deceive,
But this is what to you I must reveal."
As Creusa seeing Delphi and its Fane
Of great Apollo thought of what was vain.

'A certain passion," said she, " was recall'd,
And which I cannot think of with much hate,"
So was this wounded stranger not appall'd,
Remembering the things he did relate.
The priest would have him shun the very street
Where first his loved Lucilla he did meet—

As Euphues Philantus thus advised,
How could he then such lame confession hear,
When even then, e'en then, old pleasures prized,
He seem'd to think of love, and not of fear?
Yea, e'en like Laurence dying would exclaim,
"For having loved I cannot now feel shame.

"How should I tear thus from my beating heart
What once appeared to ope the bliss of Heav'n,
What once a belief in God did e'en impart?
Such ruthless power is to me not given."
The holy man himself seem'd quite aghast
At what between them both had lately pass'd.

Oh! what would not be urged by scoffers now?
What by the learned, contemplative, grave?
How could a priest such sheer abuse allow?
How could such bold avowals sinners save?

Think of the consequences that must follow.
Think of the hope audacious and the hollow.

Perhaps all this he too had thought of well;
But in the holy pale are thinkers then,
Who have mysterious secrets words can't tell,
Who know that God has not the thoughts of men.
" Enough," Saint Bernard answer'd, " let him die
Housell'd, anneal'd: for him the life on high."

Euffridas, Cologne's dean, used oft to sit
With those who public penance would endure,
Whose thoughts the while perhaps were never writ,
To read to, and console the struggling poor;
To ask their prayers, as if he knew that they
To God's great mercy well had found the way[1].

No public penance marks our present life,
Perhaps not e'en the sacramental known;
But Nature will impose her private strife,
Whose bitterness those long astray will own;
With outward beauty clad, abroad they stray,
Yet find to Heav'n by tears a secret way.

For " uninvestigable and unknown,"
Cries Suso, " is God's merciful abyss
To saints when perfected, who ever own
That e'er to fathom all its depths they miss,"
Which gently suffers Circumstance to rise,
And ask for pity from All-seeing eyes.

[1] Liv. vi.

The knowledge of conditions, as in God,
Implying that He knows how each man would,
On all the paths by human feet e'er trod,
Have acted if by circumstance he could,
May oft bespeak a merciful decree
Where wishes whole or half were known to be.

So even here might wonder oft begin,
Could we but know the views to which are led
Some who have stay'd to parley with their sin,
And others who appear'd to Heav'n long sped.
Through dark, wild covers bursts th' Elysian fair,
While open pastures yield no passage there.

Saint Bruno and Saint Francis, Martin old,
Guevara, and the maid of Escobar,
Have said what in this chant may not be told,
Passing beyond what some call prudence fair,
To show the visions yielded on this earth
To those in whose great weakness they had birth,

Who wander long perhaps through deserts wide,
Transform'd, too, as the ancient poets feign;
'Midst precipices, slopes, and woods they bide,
Lured by some fancy that proves wholly vain,
With faith, but nothing else to correspond;
While each, Erichthon-like, must oft despond.

" Poor sinners " are the words of ancient times,
For those accused by Belial, sent from Hell
To sue 'gainst Mercy's seat, to punish crimes,
As old French books of " consolation " tell.

The sound alone of that deep epithet
Those who deserved to hear it can't forget.

" From Sion's mount will Raab not be driven ;"
'Tis Ives de Chartres who proclaims the fact ;
Bright Heav'n is view'd by those who thus are
    shriven ;
Such bliss belongs to all who thus will act ;
As when the Magdalen had pour'd out tears,
And first to her then our risen Lord appears.

O poets wing'd ! O men for whom our hearts
Are often grieved, whom others harshly blame !
O Shelley, Byron, foremost in the arts
Of melody, deserving endless fame !
See what a portal opes for each mistake,
See how the fallen rise, and for whose sake !

O soft, frail heart ! O woman to whom Love
Has thrown it open, closed to all the proud,
Fly, laden with thy faults, and soar above,
And leave a heavy, leaden, useless shroud,
To dance on earth with that seraphic glee
Which, without other wings, brings Heav'n to
    thee !

Affinities peculiar to the frail—
Ah, may we dare to urge on taking leave ?
The neighbourhood of Heav'n we would hail.
So close and true as never to deceive ;
For God, who crime must hate and ever will,
Most dearly loves our human nature still.

Men their own works destroy, and oft disdain;
Their fondest titles will be changed to vile;
Their "Pearls of the East" will not long remain;
Dissolv'd they lasted but a little while;
But "works of his own hands," the Psalmist cries,
By prayer implying, "God will not despise."

But is it always crime in those we see
To-day so cheerful, hoping against hope,
To-morrow, perhaps, steep'd in misery,
Alone, unfriended, left their way to grope?
That cheerfulness may have a blessed spring,
That misery a wholesome, needful sting.

And sparkling words of idiomatic charm,
With frankness, courage, sprightliness, and glee,
At times can even censure just disarm,
Evincing such a spirit, noble, free,
From which all falsehood needs must swift depart,
Shamed by the presence of a truthful heart.

Who knows? what storms our pardon upon earth,
As foe to all that basely would beguile,
Can elsewhere even yield some food for mirth,
Of an unknown and, doubtless, purer style,
For where is banish'd wholly proud pretence,
There needs must be a dash of Innocence.

Perhaps, if all were known, 'tis seldom they
Have led their lovers to consort with doubt;
For though on them their crimes apostates lay,
What makes hearts happy they have long found out.

They wish'd the love of God should still endure;
Besides, then love for them would be more sure.

They loved, but would instinctively refrain
From blighting any flower that they smelt;
They never sought a noble mind to stain,
Superior to their own, they humbly felt.
They knew too well how one bright grace might
 fall,
But never would they therefore give up all.

The word "illaudable" does not apply,
At least with a Virgilian depth of sense,
To those who love, or without love will sigh,
Whatever be grammarians' vain pretence,
Who knew not when they that objection raised,
That these, at least, for somewhat can be praised.

Their future sun may shine already there,
Their present gleams may owe to it their rise;
It is not they who have invoked despair,
Or 'gainst the charm of goodness closed their eyes.
'Twixt shame and sanctity they share a bliss,
Reserved, while man disdains them, e'en for this.

For are there not reflections in the air?
Anticipated lights we know not whence?
Aurora's steeds to question who will dare,
Though sable night may seem to bid them hence?
The ground may still be darken'd to the eye,
While the lark mounts and only sees the sky.

Stern moralists may argue and contend;
Those loving her may strive to hide a tear;
The world that tempts will never her defend;
The saints on earth see darkly things with fear;
But Woman, somehow, will not trust that glass,
And o'er her own faith-lit heart will Heav'n pass.

There once was raised a temple, as we know,
" Of women to the Fortune," proudly named,
When soft Valeria and the rest did go,
And by their prayers the hero fierce was tamed,
Who led the Volsci back from frighten'd Rome,
And saved for all their country and their home.

Ah! who could count the temples now that hear
The woman's voice, the cry unheard by man,
That witness, what she seeks to hide, the tear,
More potent, which accomplish all things can
For others and herself, which should be named
" To God, not Fortune," and for ever famed.

Let others now be silent in her praise,
Let them most basely of her sins complain,
To her own Fortune she a voice will raise,
Not to a fancied Deity, and vain—
That silent voice is heard by God on high,
The woman conquers, and her shame will die.

Cæsarius urges instances in proof;
The grave De Ligny even is more bold;
For " rigorists," he says, " did keep aloof
From our sweet Lord, with harden'd hearts and
    cold;

'Gainst whom they nourish'd secret, deadly hate;
While sinners at His feet did love and wait."

But as when He by them was cherish'd so,
It may be seen no less around us here;
And thus the streams of Paradise will flow,
And all its blissful groves and lawns appear
Upon this very earth, from which will rise
Those once deem'd lost, now angels of the skies.

Genius did once two characters portray—
One always wrong, the other always right;
And in the end what is it they display?
A hero, and a wretch as black as night.
Men judged by what was hidden and made known;
And ne'er was mortal truth more nobly shown.

Ah, well I do remember me of one,
A vested Priest who at the altar stood,
Who wish'd to teach the crown some sinner won;
Some recent case unhappy touch he would.
His voice was tremulous, his look was strange,
He seem'd through worlds of love in mind to range.

And then he ceased abruptly, could not speak;
Struck dumb as if by visions, and grown faint—
Such tenderness evincing for the weak,
While all who knew him recognized the saint;
So, turning from the people once again,
To God alone he raised the holy strain.

With arms extended, soft was heard his voice,
Intoning "Credo." He had ceased to see
All but the seats of angels who rejoice,
Lost in the glories of Divinity.
So Heav'n before the multitude was shown,
The way with love's tears from one poor heart strewn.

Alack-a-day! how little do we know
The hearts of others, blinded by our pride!
How little all the tears that seek to flow,
Which modesty, not harden'd guilt, will hide!
And tears that flow not! who will dare deny
That depth profound which yet reflects the sky?

As the dark waters 'neath some woody glade,
On which the wither'd leaves are falling fast,
Such is the fair one's heart too often made,
Strewn with fond thoughts of what is ever past;
While art arrests them and prevents their flow
To the deep gulphs where only weeds do grow.

But of that pool, so calm with verdant shade,
Let but the sluice be drawn, and you will find
How forth it gushes as a torrent made;
And such presents an image of her mind,
Whose pent-up sorrow quickly disappears,
And all is cover'd by her falling tears.

But in those tears what sparkling light will shine!
Each drop seems Eden's dew, from Eden's sky,
It is that she has caught the ray Divine
Which makes it sweet to live, as erst to die

Had been her fond, sad, and desponding thought,
When to blush out her rest of life she sought.

Such have I known, now gentlest of the fair,
Once steep'd in sorrow, reckless, hopeless, wild;
A hand was stretch'd—there breathed on her an air
Which changed her to the former happy child;
To comfort others then her life was bent,
Through Heav'n on earth, like Innocence, she went.

Ah, yes, let virtue proud, to Heav'n but blind,
Assert her fancied right, these frail disdain,
But to the view of that poor scornëd mind
Th' Elysian groves are open once again;
The dark, sad thickets of her life are past;
She feels she is on earth at rest at last.

> A certain Hermit raised his cell
> Upon a hill-side, near a well,
> Where a vast forest spreading round,
> Became a most sinistrous ground.
> For it was known by deeds that there
> A noted brigand had his lair.
> Him the wise man of God did meet,
> And with sweet words, as from Heav'n, greet.
> He preach'd so well that on the spot
> The brigand vow'd to change his lot.
> So, having there confess'd his sin,
> He said a new life he'd begin.
> But all the hermit bade him then,
> Was to do good to other men

As far as he was able ever,
And then to tell a falsehood never.
The robber, being thus resolved,
Soon found the blissful problem solved.
For through the forest as he walk'd,
And with his heart transformëd talk'd,
With hands behind their backs still tied,
Bound to a tree, he then descried
Two travellers, whom outlaws there
Had left thus naked to the air.
To them, unbound, he gave a part
Of his own raiment, though the smart
Of his right eye, pierced by a bough
While speeding to them, he felt now—
So unlike those whose present pain
Will make best resolutions vain.
Some moments after, he perceived
A leper to be there relieved,
Who, still his onward way to keep,
Had found the stream he'd cross too deep,
When the late brigand plunged to swim,
And to the bank opposed brought him;
Whom he embraced, and, with a kiss,
Said, opening his purse, "Take this,"
Which then was all that he had left,
While feeling rich, and not bereft.
Soon afterwards there came in view
Two knights, that bade him stand and rue;
For by the signs, to them just sent,
They thought that he was whom was meant

As having their own brother slain;
So there they told him to remain,
And say whether he was or not
The wretch whose deed was not forgot.
The penitent, remembering well
His charge that he the truth should tell,
Replied that he was that fell clown;
And on the spot they smote him down;
While he forgave them from his heart;
And so his bright spirit did depart,
With angels to escort his soul,
Whose joyful cries recount the whole.
'Tis said the hermit, scandalized
At such an end was much surprised.
But the old minstrel told his tale,
To show how mercy can prevail
To cancel sins, and make men feel
What Heav'n so often will reveal,
That those who for all faults will sigh,
Have here Heav'n in view, and Heav'n nigh.
Oh, let those twined around your heart,
Now think like angels! so depart.

www.ingramcontent.com/pod-product-compliance
Lightning Source LLC
Chambersburg PA
CBHW031341230426
43670CB00006B/403